A Mother's Prayer

The Stuff They Don't Tell You,

The Good, The Bad, and The Caffeine

Thobekile Finger

A MOTHER'S PRAYER

Publisher Information

America Publishers
Email: info@americapublishers.com
Phone: +1 (346) 200-4098

ISBN Information

eBook: 978-1-966198-20-8
Paperback: 979-8-9998029-6-5
Hardcover: 978-1-966198-22-2

Cover Design by: America Publishers

Printed in the United States of America

1st Edition: August, 2025

FOREWORD

South Africa faces many challenges across all sectors, affecting people of all ages, genders, and backgrounds. These challenges, while experienced in different ways, are shaped by the persistent and widespread problems of poverty, inequality, and unemployment.

Young people, whether they are engaged in education, employment, or training, or are outside of these systems, are deeply influenced by the political, economic, social, and technological environments in which they live. To navigate this complex reality, they need appropriate and relevant knowledge, skills, and attitudes. Education, both basic and higher, plays a vital role in shaping the lives of young people as well as adults.

This book focuses strongly on the lives of young people in higher education, yet its lessons reach far beyond that setting. It is a practical guide for caring for young people and addresses the many factors that influence success in education. Educational institutions often reflect the societies from which students come, which means that challenges such as gender-based violence and femicide are as present in institutions as they are in communities.

The book also addresses other pressing issues, including alcohol and drug abuse, using relatable and realistic examples. The author's problem-solving approach, combined with her experience in higher education and holistic health, provides valuable guidance for supporting the psychosocial, spiritual, and physical well-being of young people. It also examines the harm caused by social exclusion, whether because of sexuality, social class, poverty, rural background, disability, or other factors, and shows how an individual's response to such exclusion can influence their success or failure.

Institutions of higher learning will find the practical advice in this book extremely useful. The content makes it clear that having policies on gender-based violence, disability, substance abuse, or financial aid is not enough. These policies need to be effectively communicated, properly implemented, and regularly reviewed. The book's examples, reflective prompts, key takeaways, and thought-provoking questions encourage readers to think critically about the issues and explore practical solutions.

Although the book was written with higher education in mind, its insights are valuable to workplaces, community centers, organizations, and families. It is a resource worth reading, discussing, and using as the basis for workshops and seminars on the important topics it raises.

By: Dr. Mvuyo Tom

ENDORSEMENT BY DR. LIZ GWYTHER

This is a remarkable book written by a remarkable woman.

It shares real-life experiences through stories developed from a survey conducted among students at higher education institutions in South Africa. Each chapter is based on an authentic story that describes specific challenges faced by students as they navigate academic commitments, social pressures, financial concerns, and other difficult situations. It also highlights personal growth, triumphs, the power of community, and the benefits of friendship, family, and mentorship.

The format of the chapters is engaging and makes the text easy to read. Each one begins with a compelling narrative that paints a vivid picture of the student, their worries, anxieties, and challenges. It shows how the student works through their problems and grows as they confront specific issues. The chapters also feature concise statements that emphasize important considerations, followed by reflective questions to guide personal thought on the topic. In addition, each chapter includes a list of resources and practical advice for readers who may be facing similar challenges in their own lives.

The target audience includes high school students planning their next steps into higher education. However, the wisdom and guidance in this book also apply to current university and college students, their parents and families, academic and administrative staff, higher education authorities, religious advisors, and schoolteachers or career counselors.

This is a deeply personal book, drawing on both the stories collected in the survey and the author's own life experiences. Thobekile Finger began her career in hospice as a professional counselor for children and families at the height of the HIV epidemic, before treatment became widely available. She currently serves as Program Director for Higher Health, an organization working with the Department of Higher Education and dedicated to student health, psychosocial well-being, and holistic youth development in South Africa. This work has uniquely prepared her to write this book. In addition to addressing the challenges of adapting to academic life, the book examines financial literacy, the impact of social media on students, the experiences of LGBTQI+ individuals, campus safety, mental health issues, disability-related challenges, and gender-based violence.

The "Mother's Prayer" in the book's title addresses gender-based violence and femicide, a shameful scourge in our country. Thobekile is a committed advocate for the safety of women and young people in the face of this crisis. Her future work in this space will be valuable in providing advice on how we can all be involved in combating this threat to our society.

This comprehensive work also celebrates the strength of community and the influence of student voices in creating positive change. It extends its reach beyond academics to discuss entrepreneurship and opportunities for earning while studying and after graduation, addressing the critical challenge of youth unemployment in South Africa.

Throughout the book, we are reminded of the importance of community. Towards the end, Thobekile also emphasizes other positive forces, such as the power of gratitude, unconditional family love, compassion, and the resilience and perseverance demonstrated by many students in these stories.

This book will touch the hearts of everyone who reads it and will serve as a valuable resource to guide young people, their parents, and their mentors. I recommend it without reservation.

PREFACE

As your child stands at the threshold of this significant milestone, transitioning from high school to college or university, it is natural to feel a mix of emotions - excitement, hope, and a hint of uncertainty. **As a mother, you want the best for your child, and this transition can be a pivotal moment in their academic and their personal journey.**

Amid preparation and planning, it is essential to acknowledge the power of prayer and navigating this transition. By combining spiritual practices with scientific approaches to goal setting, stress management, and resilience-building, you can provide your child with a holistic foundation for success.

This book is a culmination of my personal and work experiences, struggles, and triumphs as a learner and a mother, and I am grateful to have had the opportunity to share it with others. It aims to support you and your child as you embark on this journey together. Within these pages, you will find practical advice, real-life examples, and inspiring stories to help your child thrive in college or university life. From navigating academic expectations to building social connections, we will explore the essential skills and strategies your child needs to succeed. As you pray for your child's successful transition, this book may be a valuable resource, offering guidance, reassurance, and inspiration. May your child's university journey be filled with purpose, passion, and promise.

I am grateful to God for the opportunity to write this book, and I thank Him for the wisdom and guidance He has provided throughout this journey. **When God Gives You a Vision, He Makes Provision. As a**

mother, there is no greater investment than praying for your child's well-being, happiness, and success.

The Mother's Prayer is a heartfelt expression of love, concern, and hope for the future. It is a personal investment in their lives, seeking guidance, protection, and blessings from a higher power. If you believe in it. Amid life's challenges, praying for your child can bring comfort, reassurance, and hope. *It is a way to show love, care, and commitment to their well-being, and to seek wisdom and guidance in navigating the complexities of life.* To the young people who have shared their stories, struggles, and triumphs with me, I thank you for your courage and vulnerability. Your experiences have enriched this book and will undoubtedly inspire and motivate others. The church has been a source of comfort, guidance, and strength for many young people and their loved ones.

To my mother, Yengiwe Manyana, my late grandparents, words can never be enough to say thank you, and to all the mothers, Aunts and Grandmothers who have prayed tirelessly for their children's success I see you. A special thank you to my husband Mosekge Finger, I thank you for your patience, encouragement, and understanding. To my sister Thobeka for your prayers, my children Thozama, Refiloe and Dumisani, my nephews and nieces Lomso, Zoey, Praise and Thathohatsiyarona for your contributions during the writing process. You have been my inspiration and shown me unconditional love. To my grandson Thandolwethu you have been my source of inspiration, when I was at my low your candid smile and laughter kept me going. To the rest of my clan, Dovana, Khumalo, Finger and the Manyana Families thank you for raising me, and shaping my character.

Family to me goes beyond my immediate family, to all those people who have touched my life and continue to do so, friends who were there throughout this journey with support and encouragement. I see you and I am eternally grateful.

To my fellow mothers, I acknowledge your unwavering commitment to your children's well-being and success. Your prayers, love, and support are the foundation upon which this book is built.

I would like to extend my deepest gratitude to the publishing and editing team and everyone who have contributed to the book, Mrs Farai Ntuli, Reverend Dr Stephen Hendricks (special thanks for contributing a chapter), Dr Mvuyo Tom, and Dr Liz Gwyther. Your expertise and dedication have brought this project to life. May this book be a blessing to young people transitioning from high school to university, and may it inspire them to trust in God's plan for their lives and their commitment to their academic journey. Organizations like Tshireletsong Place of Safety Naledi Hospice in Bloemfontein South Africa have played a significant role in shaping my professional trajectory and igniting my passion for supporting vulnerable youth.

My journey in writing "The Mother's Prayer" has been deeply influenced by my experiences working with young people in underprivileged communities. As Psychosocial Development Officer at Naledi Hospice, and Project Development Specialist for Care and support at the United States Agency for International Development (USAID), I witnessed the **transformative power of palliative care**, which focuses on holistic care and support for individuals and families affected by life threatening illness. Palliative care's emphasis on addressing physical, emotional, and spiritual needs resonated with me, and I saw firsthand its impact on improving quality of life.

TABLE OF CONTENTS

Chapter 3: Campus Safety 101 - What Every Student Should Know

Chapter 1:

There is a Purpose in the Detour

Chomi, The Struggle is Real!

The sun rose gently over the large campus, casting a warm golden glow on the neatly trimmed lawns and tall buildings. For Nokuthula, this day was more than just the start of university—it was the weight of her family's dreams pressing on her shoulders. Every step through the towering campus gates felt like entering a new world, both exciting and a little scary.

She stepped through the main gates, clutching her well-worn backpack tightly against her chest. The chatter of learners, the rustle of papers, and the occasional burst of laughter surrounded her, yet she felt strangely detached as if she was just watching from the sidelines. The campus was vibrant alive with energy, but to her, it felt like a maze of unfamiliar places.

Coming from a small village, this university was more than just education for Nokuthula; it was a lifeline. Her family had made sacrifices to send her here, and now their hopes rested squarely on her shoulders.

Standing awkwardly beyond the gates, her heart hammered in her chest. The iron gates stood tall, gleaming in blue and gold under the afternoon sun. Students moved through them in a rhythmic flow— chatter mixing with the crunch of gravel under hurried footsteps. Some students walked confidently in groups, others with headphones in, lost in their own worlds. A wave of nervous energy rushed through her. She shifted her weight from one foot to the other, suddenly aware of how heavy her bag felt on her back. A group of students brushed past her, their laughter sharp and easy, as if they already belonged here. Nokuthula's throat tightened. She had dreamt of this moment for years—being part of a university, walking these very halls—but now that it was real, it felt too big. Too loud. Too much.

A strong, brief burst of wind blew her braids across her face. She tucked them behind her ear and took a deep breath to steady herself. Just a few steps forward. That's all she needed to do. Her mother's words echoed in her mind: *"God wouldn't have brought you this far just to leave you."*

Slowly, she crossed the threshold. The chatter of students surrounded her—carefree voices and casual jokes—but none of it touched her. Her eyes scanned the surroundings, searching for a familiar face, but all she saw were strangers. The confident stride of a senior student. The careless shrug of a girl balancing three books on her hip. The easy handshake between two friends.

Nokuthula inhaled deeply. *One step at a time.* She reminded herself that this was where she was meant to be. That she belonged here.

As Nokuthula stood there, feeling strangely distant from the lively campus around her, a warm voice broke through her thoughts.

"Hi there! Are you new here?"

She turned to see a young woman with a kind smile and a welcoming demeanor.

"I'm Zanele," she introduced herself, extending a hand.

"You look a bit lost. Let me show you around."

Zanele's excitement was contagious.

As she pointed to the library, she said with a grin, "That library? I basically live there during exam season. First-year assignments are no joke!"

She pointed at the canteen, adding, "And if you ever need a caffeine boost, this is the place. Their coffee and Amangwinya (Fat Cakes) are lifesavers during finals."

Nokuthula found herself smiling for the first time that day.

"I think I'll be needing a lot of coffee," she replied shyly, earning a laugh from Zanele.

"Don't worry," Zanele said, her tone warm. "You're going to love it here—you just need to give yourself time to settle in."

As she walked away, Nokuthula felt a small but comforting sense of relief. Zanele's warmth had shown her that even in a place where everything felt new, she wouldn't be entirely alone. Thinking of the library's quiet refuge and the lingering aroma of caramel lattes, she stepped into the main building. This wasn't just her journey—it was her family's, too. Their sacrifices had brought her here, and she wouldn't let them go to waste. She took a deep breath. No matter what lay ahead, she was ready to face it.

The Weight of Expectations

In her village, Nokuthula was more than just a student—she was a symbol of hope, the first in her family to enter the world of higher education. Her mother's voice lingered in her mind, a blend of pride and quiet fear:

"You carry all our dreams with you, my girl. Make us proud."

As uplifting as those words were, they felt like a heavy crown on her head. The night before she left home, her mother had lit a small candle, its flickering light dancing across the modest walls. They sat in heavy silence, the weight of unspoken words filling the room. Finally, her mother spoke, her voice steady but filled with emotion.

"You are a gift, Nokuthula," she said, taking her hand.

"This is your chance to break the cycle, to give us all a reason to believe that things can be better. Promise me you'll never give up, no matter how hard it gets."

Her mother's words reminded Nokuthula of another voice that had shaped her journey—her grandfather's. He had never learned to read or write, yet through sheer determination, he had built a thriving business from nothing. Nokuthula's mother often recounted his story: how he had created opportunities with nothing but his hands and unshakable faith in himself.

"You come from strong people," her mother would remind her.

As Nokuthula unpacked in her residence room, her fingers traced the smooth curves of her grandfather's wooden carving—a small, simple figure that carried deep meaning. He had given it to her during one of her moments of self-doubt, saying, "Even the smallest tools can create something remarkable if you work hard enough."

This carving now sat on her desk, a silent witness to her struggles and a symbol of resilience. But balancing her family's dreams with her own aspirations was a challenge. The weight of expectations pressed down on her, the fear of failure never far behind.

Every day, Nokuthula grappled with the two sides of her journey— gratitude for the opportunity and the weight of expectations. Her family's sacrifices pushed her forward, but they also weighed her down. Could she truly carry the dreams of so many on her shoulders?

Reflection Prompt:

- What kind of a person do I want to become during my college or university life journey, what are my non-negotiables, and how will I prioritize them?

- Think of a time when your family or community supported you through a difficult challenge, write about how their sacrifices or encouragement inspired you.

- Then, create a list of three ways you can actively honor their efforts—whether through small daily habits, achieving a personal goal, or giving back to your community.

- How can you set boundaries and assert your independence while still respecting your parents' wishes?

The Reality Check: Financial Setbacks

The first week at university was a blur—exciting, overwhelming, and surprisingly costly. However, the joy of being in this environment was quickly replaced by the harsh realities of financial strain. Each step she took on campus reminded her of how much everything cost—the textbooks with their glossy covers that seemed out of reach, the canteen meals priced like luxuries, and even the cost of transportation to and from her residence. Every expense felt like a burden weighing down her dreams.

Her mother's voice, both soothing and strained, crackled over the phone: "We'll manage, my girl. We always do."

But Nokuthula knew what "managing" often meant for her family— going without. Whether it was skipping meals or borrowing from neighbors, her family's sacrifices were tangible, and she couldn't ignore the guilt that came with knowing they were stretching themselves thin to support her.

Determined to ease the burden, she began searching the campus for part-time work opportunities. Nokuthula spent hours scanning notice boards and jotting down potential leads.

"Tutor needed for high school Maths students," one flyer read.

"Library assistant position available," another claimed.

Yet, despite her eagerness, most opportunities required prior experience or connections she didn't have. Each rejection chipped away at her confidence, but she refused to give up.

Weeks passed, and her savings dwindled, but her determination never wavered. One day, after what felt like endless searching, Nokuthula found herself in a small canteen just off campus. A *"Help Wanted!"* sign taped to the window caught her eye, and she walked in, clutching her CV tightly. The manager barely glanced at it.

"Can you start tomorrow?"

Her voice was brisk, her eyes scanning the busy canteen, already moving on to the next task.

The job was far from glamorous. The canteen never slept. Orders barked from the kitchen, trays wobbling under the weight of steaming cups, customers tapping their fingers impatiently. Nokuthula barely had time to breathe, her muscles aching, her mind spinning between school and survival. Her feet ached at the end of every shift, and the late nights often bled into her study hours. But every paycheck she received brought a small sense of relief, a concrete symbol of her effort to contribute.

On some nights, exhaustion left her staring at her unfinished assignments, her hands too heavy to turn the pages. In those moments, she turned to Psalm 55:22: *"Cast your burden on the Lord, and He will sustain you."*

As she whispered the words aloud, she felt her anxiety ease. These moments of prayer didn't just comfort her—they gave her clarity. With her mind at peace, she decided to take action, researching bursaries and organizing a support group for learners like herself. Her faith transformed her perspective, showing her that each challenge was an opportunity to trust and grow.

One evening, after a particularly exhausting shift, she collapsed into a chair in the canteen's back room, her arms heavy from carrying trays all night. Her colleague, Lunga, walked in and raised an eyebrow.

"Rough night?" he asked, leaning against the counter.

She nodded, letting out a tired sigh.

"I feel like I'm drowning. There's just so much to balance."

Lunga smirked. "You're still here, aren't you? That means you've got more fight in you than you realize." He pointed to her name badge.

"The fact that you're still here means you've got what it takes."

His words stayed with her, settling deep like a seed. Maybe, just maybe, she was stronger than she thought.

Lunga's words echoed in Nokuthula's mind long after that grueling shift. His quiet confidence in her sparked a change, pushing her past survival mode and into action. With his encouragement as a catalyst, she began taking small but meaningful steps to improve her situation.

Despite the demanding hours at the canteen, Nokuthula knew she needed more financial support. Late at night, after endless canteen shifts, she went through scholarship applications, her fatigue battling with her determination. Through trial and error, she uncovered ways to lighten the financial burden—not just for herself but for others like her.

Practical Tip:

When facing financial challenges as a learner/student, consider these resources:

- **Bursaries and Scholarships:** Check your institution's website for need-based and merit-based scholarships. Many private organizations also offer specialized bursaries for underserved communities.

- **Student Financial Aid:** Apply for government student loans or grants, such as NSFAS in South Africa or Pell Grants in the U.S., which often include provisions for living expenses.

- **Part-Time Jobs:** Explore opportunities on campus (library assistant, tutoring, or administrative roles) or in the local community (canteens, retail, or events). Platforms like Indeed and university job boards often list student-friendly jobs.

- **Community Support:** Contact local community centers or faith-based organizations for small grants or financial aid.

- **Crowdfunding:** Platforms like GoFundMe can help raise funds for tuition or essential expenses, especially if paired with a compelling story.

Small steps like these can alleviate financial stress and empower you to focus on your academic goals.

With these strategies in mind and guidance from a campus counselor, Nokuthula applied for multiple funding opportunities. Her efforts didn't just help her; they inspired others. She started sharing resources with her peers, creating a small network of learners who supported one another by exchanging tips and leads for part-time work or financial aid. What started as a solo fight became something bigger— a network of students, all lifting each other up, proving that no one had to struggle alone.

These financial setbacks, while daunting, taught her invaluable lessons about resilience, resourcefulness, and the power of community. She realized that success wasn't just about academic achievements—it was about perseverance and the ability to navigate life's challenges with determination.

Even as paychecks trickled in, the weight of financial stress never left her. It clung to her, pressing against every decision she made. It wasn't just the physical exhaustion from long shifts at the canteen or the stress of balancing her schedule—it was the constant worry about whether she was doing enough. These thoughts lingered long after her shifts ended, following her back to her residence like an unwelcome shadow.

The financial strain magnified her feelings of isolation. Laughter echoed from the common room; invitations floated past her, but Nokuthula hesitated. A single meal out could mean a week of instant noodles—so she stayed in, her room becoming both a sanctuary and a prison. This sense of being on the outside looking in began to take an emotional toll, feeding into her growing homesickness and self-doubt.

Alone at her residence, staring at the unfamiliar city lights outside, she wondered: *Where did she truly belong?*

Reflection Prompt:

- Identify a specific financial challenge you're facing right now (e.g., budgeting, affording a course, or saving for a need).

- Write down two small, realistic steps you can take this week to address it, like researching scholarships or creating a simple budget plan.

- Reflect on how these steps will bring you closer to your goals.

Rebuilding: Finding Strength and Support

The weight of financial stress and homesickness pressed down on Nokuthula, growing heavier each day. The thought of quitting whispered to her—a quiet temptation promising escape from the tiredness. Progress felt like an illusion; every step forward seemed to dissolve beneath her feet. The challenges towered over her, and giving up started to feel like the only way out.

One rainy afternoon, Nokuthula sat in the far corner of the library, her open textbook forgotten beneath her trembling hands. Raindrops traced uneven paths down the windowpane, the sound dull and rhythmic against the glass. Around her, students whispered and flipped through papers, their quiet focus making her feel even more isolated.

Ms. Dlamini's voice broke through the fog. "You look like you're carrying the weight of the world on your shoulders."

Nokuthula lifted her gaze, her eyes heavy with unspilled tears. Ms. Dlamini pulled out a chair and settled into it, her expression calm but attentive.

"I can't keep up," Nokuthula confessed, her voice barely rising above the library's muted hum. "Every time I think I'm making progress, something pulls me back under. I'm drowning."

Ms. Dlamini's hand rested gently on Nokuthula's arm. "Do you know what I see when I look at you?" Her tone was measured but warm. "I see someone who's already fought harder than most to get here. Struggles don't define you, Nokuthula—it's the strength to stand back up that matters."

Nokuthula's chest tightened. "But what if I fail?" Her voice trembled with doubt.

Ms. Dlamini smiled knowingly. "Success isn't a straight road," she said. "It's messy—full of wrong turns and unexpected stops. But if you keep moving, you'll find your way."

She leaned in slightly. "When I was in your shoes, I wanted to quit too. But then I thought about my mother—how hard she worked to put me through school. Giving up would have meant throwing away everything she sacrificed. So, I took it one day at a time. And eventually, things started to shift."

Nokuthula wiped a tear from her cheek. "But how do I keep going?"

"Start with small victories," Ms. Dlamini replied. "Write down one thing you accomplish each day, even if it's something as simple as finishing an assignment or asking a question in class. You'll see—the small wins build up over time."

That evening, Nokuthula opened her journal, the glow from her desk lamp casting soft shadows across the page. She hesitated for a moment, then wrote: "*Completed my assignment today. Spoke up in class.*"

The next day, she added more: "*Helped Zanele with her notes. Understood the reading for the first time.*"

With each entry, her confidence strengthened. Small victories turned into quiet triumphs. The weight of uncertainty didn't disappear—but step by step, Nokuthula was learning how to carry it.

Emotional and Social Adjustments

Nokuthula had imagined university as a place of discovery and freedom—a place where she could finally step into her own life. But instead, it felt like a vast, unfamiliar world where she was merely an observer.

The canteen buzzed with conversations she wasn't part of, the rise and fall of voices mixing with the clatter of trays and the scrape of metal chairs against the floor. Across the room, a group of girls leaned toward each other, laughing as one of them scrolled through her phone. A boy tossed a crumpled napkin toward a friend, who caught it mid-air with a grin. Nokuthula stirred her tea, the warmth of the cup fading against her palms. She had dreamt of this place—of study sessions, late-night talks, and friendships that felt effortless. But the reality was different. The conversations around her were fast and sharp, the inside jokes unknown to her. She smiled faintly when someone made eye contact, but no one lingered long enough to invite her in.

Homesickness was an ever-present ache tucked beneath her ribcage. She missed the sound of her mother's morning prayers drifting through the thin walls of their house and the creak of the front gate when her brother ran home from school. She missed the weight of her father's hand on her shoulder after evening prayers and the quiet hum of her grandfather carving wood beneath the old peech tree.

One afternoon, she sat at a crowded table in the library. A girl beside her flipped through a stack of papers, leaning toward her friend with a whispered laugh. Nokuthula adjusted her notebook, her heart thudding painfully in her chest. *Just say something*, she told herself. *Anything*. But the words stuck in her throat, and the conversation continued without her. That night, she sat at her desk, the soft glow of her lamp casting long shadows on the walls. Her journal lay open before her, and the ink smudged where her hand had remained.

Lord, guide me to the right people. Help me to feel at home here. The words spilled out of her as tears welled in her eyes. Slowly, journaling became her refuge—a quiet place where she could make sense of the loneliness pressing down on her. She often wondered if she had made the right choice in leaving home for a life that felt so foreign and overwhelming.

At lunch, she hovered near a table of classmates, gripping the strap of her bag. *Just say something*, she urged herself. *A joke. A greeting. Anything*. Once again, the words caught in her throat. Before she could decide, they erupted into laughter at an inside joke, sealing the invisible wall between them. Nokuthula turned away, her heart sinking.

Each night, when the loneliness crept in, Nokuthula reached for her journal. Her shaky handwriting traced out whispered prayers, sometimes ending with tears staining the ink. It wasn't just a place for reflection—it was where she held herself together. Each entry ended with a verse that resonated with her struggles, like Isaiah 41:10: *"Fear not, for I am with you; be not dismayed, for I am your God."* One night, feeling particularly isolated, she wrote: *"Lord, guide me to the right people. Help me build connections that bring joy and support."*

At night, when the residence was quiet, Nokuthula would pour her thoughts onto its pages. She wrote about her fears, her doubts, and the small moments of hope that occasionally pierced through the darkness. Journaling wasn't just a coping mechanism; it became a way for her to reconnect with her inner strength and reflect on the reasons she had come so far.

The next day, she found herself sitting beside a group of classmates, introducing herself with a hesitant smile. That small act of faith-inspired courage marked the beginning of meaningful friendships.

A turning point came during her communication class. The lecturer had assigned a group project—designing a campaign to promote mental health awareness among students. Nokuthula was nervous but determined. When she joined her group for their first meeting, she spoke cautiously, afraid that her ideas might be dismissed. To her surprise, her teammates listened intently, nodding in agreement as she shared her thoughts.

As the project progressed, the group grew closer. Late-night brainstorming sessions in the common room were filled with laughter, shared snacks, and a growing sense of camaraderie. Nokuthula found herself opening up, laughing along with them, and even leading discussions. One night, as they finalized their presentation, someone joked about their frantic last-minute efforts. The room erupted into laughter—the kind that makes your cheeks ache and tears well up in your eyes.

As laughter filled the room, Nokuthula leaned back, taking it all in. This wasn't just about a project anymore. It was proof—that she belonged, that she had a voice, and that she was more than just a girl struggling to fit in. For the first time since she arrived, she felt light, like maybe—just maybe—she had found her place.

Volunteering at the campus support center became another lifeline. Nokuthula met students who shared similar struggles—those navigating homesickness, academic pressure, and the strain of being away from home. Together, they built a safe space where they could share stories, exchange advice, and simply support one another. Through these interactions, Nokuthula began to realize that her feelings of doubt and isolation weren't unique—they were part of the universal experience of stepping out of one's comfort zone.

By the end of the semester, Nokuthula had built a small but meaningful network of friends and supporters. These relationships didn't erase her homesickness or her insecurities, but they gave her the strength to keep going. Slowly, she began to see the campus not as a daunting maze but as a place filled with opportunities for growth and connection.

Personal Safety

The campus was quieter at night. The chatter of the day faded into silence, broken only by the occasional hum of a passing car. Nokuthula's footsteps echoed along the pavement as she walked back to her residence. She adjusted the strap of her backpack and glanced over her shoulder. The path behind her was empty—but the quiet felt suffocating.

Her fingers tightened around her phone. Zanele's words came back to her:

"Always keep your phone charged and share your location with someone you trust."

Nokuthula had smiled at the time, brushing it off as unnecessary advice—but not anymore.

One evening, a shadow followed her from the library. At first, she thought it was nothing—just another student walking in the same direction. But when she quickened her pace, the footsteps behind her matched the rhythm. Her chest tightened. A cold knot formed in her stomach.

She had spotted a group of students ahead—talking and laughing as they crossed toward the residence. Without thinking, she stepped into their space, flowing with their conversation. She forced a smile and walked with them until the shadow behind her disappeared into the night.

After that night, Nokuthula started paying closer attention to her surroundings. She memorized the well-lit paths and avoided the shortcuts through the side alleys. If she stayed late in the library, she walked back with Zanele or called a friend to stay on the phone with her until she was safely home.

Safety, she realized, wasn't about fear—it was about confidence and preparation. Small habits made a difference. Keeping her phone charged, walking in groups, and sticking to well-lit areas weren't signs of weakness—they were quiet acts of strength.

Be alert but not afraid. That's what Zanele had told her. Nokuthula still carried the weight of uncertainty, but with each passing day, she learned to trust herself more. Strength wasn't about never feeling fear— it was about knowing how to respond when it appeared.

Responsibility for Your Own Safety

One evening, after a late study session, Nokuthula noticed how quiet the campus paths were. The shadows beneath the streetlights seemed to stretch longer. She quickened her pace, clutching her bag. Zanele's words echoed in her mind: "*Always keep your phone charged and share your location with someone you trust.*" Safety, she realized, wasn't just about luck—it was about preparation. She learned to trust her instincts, stay alert during late walks back to her She had spotted a group of students ahead—talking and laughing as they crossed toward the residence avoiding isolated areas.

Small habits, like walking with a friend after dark and staying aware of her surroundings, became part of her daily routine. Developing these habits gave her a sense of control, a quiet reassurance that she could navigate this new environment with strength and awareness.

- Think of one instance where you felt lonely or unsure in a new environment. How did you respond? Now, brainstorm three specific actions you can take this week to build connections— like joining a study group, introducing yourself to a classmate, or attending a campus event.

- Reflect on how these actions could create opportunities for friendship and support.

Living beyond Circumstances

Some nights, exhaustion clung to her like a thick blanket. Her body ached from hours of standing at the canteen, her eyes burned from studying past midnight, and her heart tightened under the never-ending worry about money. University had always been her dream, but lately, it felt like survival. Was she strong enough to keep going? Balancing academics, part-time work, and her emotional well-being felt like juggling weights instead of balls, each one threatening to slip from her grasp. Yet, in the midst of the chaos, she discovered an inner strength that she hadn't known she possessed—a resilience born from her circumstances.

A turning point came when her aunt offered her a part-time job selling clothes at the weekend market. At first, Nokuthula hesitated. She was already stretched thin, and the thought of adding another responsibility felt overwhelming. But her financial situation left her with little choice. The work was physically demanding—early mornings spent hauling heavy bags, setting up stalls, and standing on her feet for hours under the scorching sun. Yet, despite the exhaustion, she found herself adapting.

The market was a world of its own—vibrant, loud, unpredictable. The air was thick with the scent of grilled maize and spices, voices overlapping as vendors called out deals. She learned quickly how to charm hesitant buyers, when to lower her price, and how to stand her ground against tough negotiators. The work was exhausting, but every sale felt like a small victory, proof that she was capable of more than she had ever believed.

After a particularly grueling day at the market, Nokuthula returned to her residence, her shoulders weighed down by fatigue. As tears welled in her eyes, she reached for her Bible, flipping through its familiar pages. That night, as weariness settled deep in her bones, she let the Bible fall open on her lap. Philippians 4:13. She traced the words with her fingers, whispering them aloud.

"I can do all things through Christ who strengthens me."

The burden on her shoulders didn't lift, but something shifted inside her—a quiet certainty. If she kept going, if she kept trusting, she would find a way. The next morning, she approached her work with renewed energy, viewing each task as an opportunity to honor her faith.

She began to see the market not just as a means to an end but as a space where she could grow. Regular customers started recognizing her, offering kind words and encouragement.

"You're a hard worker," an elderly woman told her with a warm smile. "That will take you far."

Her resilience spilled over into her academic life. She applied for bursaries and scholarships, dedicating late nights to perfecting her applications. She joined study groups, finding support and accountability among peers who were also navigating the complexities of university life. Slowly but surely, she began to find a balance.

She once thought resilience was about pushing through, about pretending the struggle didn't hurt. But now she understood resilience was about choosing to rise, even when everything felt overwhelming. It was in the small choices—the late-night study sessions, the early mornings at the market, the whispered prayers in the quiet of her room.

She couldn't control everything. But she could control how she moved forward. And that was enough.

Reflection Prompt:

- Identify one major challenge you're facing that feels overwhelming (e.g., balancing work and studies, managing family responsibilities).

- Write down a clear, actionable step you can take this week to begin tackling it, such as setting a small daily goal or seeking advice from a mentor.

- Reflect on how achieving this step will impact your overall progress.

Key Takeaways from This Chapter

Adjusting to College or University Life Takes Time – It's normal to feel overwhelmed at first. Give yourself time to adapt to the new environment, routines, and expectations.

Financial Planning is Key – Managing tuition, accommodation, and daily expenses requires budgeting and exploring scholarships or part-time job opportunities.

Balance Freedom with Responsibility – College and university offer independence, but success depends on how well you manage your time, priorities, and commitments.

Seek Support When Needed – Utilize campus resources such as academic advisors, counseling services, and peer support groups to help navigate challenges.

Stay Focused on Your Goals – Social life is important, but staying committed to your academic journey will set you up for future success.

Navigating college or university can feel daunting, especially for first-time students like Nokuthula. Many learners face challenges in adjusting to academic expectations, financial responsibilities, and personal independence. To help students prepare, I have included this 'College & University Starter Pack'—a practical guide with essential tips on registration, financial planning, personal wellness, and Residence essentials.

"Whether you are just starting your college or university journey or looking for ways to manage your experience better, this guide will provide actionable insights to make your transition smoother."

COLLEGE & UNIVERSITY STARTER PACK

1. **Pre-Registration**

   - Research institution
   - Explore universities and Technical Vocational Education and Training TVETs Colleges
     - Choose a program
     - Select desired courses/degrees and ensure they align with your interests, abilities, and career goals.
   - Check admission requirements
     - Verify necessary documents, grades, and exams (e.g., APS, SAT, ACT, or matriculation exams).
   - Apply for financial aid
   - Explore scholarships, grants, loans, and bursaries.

2. **Registration and Administration**

   - Complete and submit applications for selected institutions and programs.
   - Register for entrance exams.

- Book and prepare for required exams (e.g., SAT, ACT, or subject-specific tests

3. **Secure accommodation**

- Apply for residence or explore off-campus housing options.

4. **Academic Preparation / Career Guidance**

- Complete prerequisite courses

- Ensure you've completed the necessary subjects and courses.

  o Your official Grade 11 or 12 results, meet with a career guidance or life orientation teacher

  o Discuss course selection, credit transfers, and academic goals.

5. **Financial Planning**

- Create a budget

- Establish a budget for tuition, living expenses, and random costs.

- Open a bank account specifically for college/university expenses.

- Explore part-time job opportunities

- Consider on-campus or off-campus part-time jobs.

6. **Technology and Equipment**

- Purchase a laptop/tablet (Obtain a suitable device for academic purposes)

- Technology and Accessories

- Power bank for extra battery life

- Headphones

- Portable hard drive or cloud storage subscription (ensure access to necessary software, tools, and subscriptions (e.g., Microsoft Office, Adobe Creative Cloud).

- Set up reliable internet and data plans for your device (Some campuses do provide WiFi)

7. Personal Care and Wellness

- Visit a primary health care clinic for a medical check-up, if you have a medical aid, consult your doctor for a full medical check-up.

- Familiarize yourself with available counseling services and support systems.

- Join student organizations and explore clubs, societies, and organizations that match your interests.

- Medications and prescriptions

- First-aid kit

- Vitamins and supplements, if budget allows

- Healthy snacks

- Water bottle

- Personal hygiene items (Towels and toiletries)

8. Final Preparations

- Confirm enrollment documents and verify your enrollment letter and course schedule.

- Attend orientation and participate in orientation programs to familiarize yourself with the campus and academic environment.

- Set academic goals and establish short-term and long-term academic goals.

9. Residences - Room Essentials

- Religious texts, Journal

- Bedding (sheets, blankets, comforter)

- Basic clothing items, hoody, shoes, and sneakers (5 T-shirts and three Jeans, depending on your style and budget are a good starter pack).

- Hangers for closet

- Laundry basket and detergents

- Desk lamp

- Comfort items (e.g., photos, plants, things that remind you of your family)
  - Mini fridge (if allowed by the institution)
  - Microwave (if allowed by the institution)

10. Financial and Administrative

- Student ID

- Bank card

- Scholarship or financial aid documents

- **NSFAS Application Essentials**
  To apply for NSFAS funding, you'll need to submit the following essential documents:

- **Personal Identification Documents**
  • Certified copy of your South African ID card or green barcoded ID book
  • Birth certificate (if you're under 18 or do not have an ID)

- **Parent/Guardian Identification**
  - Certified copies of your parent(s) or legal guardian(s)' ID documents
- **Proof of Income**
  - Recent payslips or an employment letter (if employed)
  - Affidavit stating employment status and income (if unemployed or self-employed)
  - Official SASSA grant letter (if your household receives social grants)
- **Academic Records**
  - Grade 12 certificate or latest school report
  - Academic transcripts (if already enrolled in tertiary education)
- **Additional Documents (if applicable)**
  - Disability Annexure A form and medical certificate (if you have a disability)
  - Vulnerable Child Declaration form (completed by a social worker)
  - Certified copy of death certificate (if a parent or guardian is deceased)
- **Proof of Residence**
  - Utility bill, rental agreement, or affidavit confirming your home address
- **Proof of Acceptance**
  - Official acceptance letter from a university or TVET college
- **Consent Form**
  - Completed and signed NSFAS consent form
- **Banking Details**
  - Bank account confirmation letter or document with your banking details

Important Note:

Ensure all documents are certified, clear, and legible. Upload them in the correct format (PDF, JPEG, or PNG) on the NSFAS online portal.

11. Academic Essentials

- Stationery
  - Notebooks and binders
  - Pens, pencils, and highlighters
  - Sticky notes and tabs
  - Index cards
- Calculator
- Flash drive

Closing: Hope for the Future

As Nokuthula walked back to her Residence one evening, the campus seemed different. The same paths she had once walked with hesitation now carried the quiet confidence of her footsteps. Where anxiety had once gripped her, there was now a calm assurance. She belonged here. The glow of study lamps from Residence windows, the hum of low murmurs from open doors, and the distant sound of laughter no longer overwhelmed her. Instead, they reminded her of how far she had come.

Her thoughts wandered back to her first day. She remembered the apprehension she felt as she stepped through the gates, clutching her backpack tightly. The fear of failure, the weight of her family's sacrifices, and the unknown future had loomed large. Now, those same fears felt smaller, dwarfed by the confidence she had built through persistence and faith.

Her grandfather's carving sat on her desk, its smooth surface catching the soft light of her desk lamp. She ran her fingers along its edges, thinking of his words: "*Even the smallest tools can create something remarkable if you work hard enough.*" The carving wasn't just a keepsake; it was a testament to her journey. It reminded her of the lessons she had learned—not just from her grandfather but from every challenge she had faced and overcome.

The financial struggles, the homesickness, the self-doubt—all of these had shaped her. They weren't just obstacles; they were the foundation of her growth. Nokuthula had learned to embrace her journey, to find strength in her faith, and to trust that every setback was an opportunity to rise stronger.

That evening, she opened her journal, a practice that had become her sanctuary, and wrote: "*The struggle is real, but so is the strength to overcome.*" These words weren't just a reflection—they were a promise. They were a reminder of the resilience that had carried her this far and would continue to guide her in the future.

Her journey was far from over. There would still be challenges ahead—tests to take, responsibilities to shoulder, and uncertainties to face. But Nokuthula no longer feared them. She welcomed them as opportunities to grow, to learn, and to keep building the life she had dreamed of.

As she sat down to plan her next steps, a sense of calm washed over her. She had stepped into this journey unsure of herself, but now she stood with purpose. The struggles hadn't broken her; they had shaped her. She wasn't just surviving—she was stepping boldly into her future, ready for whatever came next. And as she closed her journal and turned off her desk lamp, she whispered a quiet prayer of gratitude—for the past, the present, and the hope that lay in the future.

Motivational Quote:

"*Every challenge you face today is shaping the person you're meant to become tomorrow.*"

Chapter 2:

You Are the Future

"Choma, Be Wise or Be Out"

Noma stepped onto the campus quad, her pulse quickening with excitement. The cool evening air buzzed with the hum of voices, accented by laughter that spilled out from nearby residences. Strings of fairy lights illuminated the space, casting a warm glow over the gathering crowd. She tugged at the hem of her sequined top, a confident smile plastered across her face, though deep down, her heart raced—not out of fear, but from the thrill of it all.

It was her first week at university, and Noma had quickly found herself swept up in the whirlwind of late-night parties and spontaneous social outings. The appeal of newfound freedom was intoxicating. No longer confined by the strict routines of her high school days, she delighted in the ability to make her own choices to live life on her own terms. The possibilities seemed endless.

"Choma, you're glowing tonight!" a friend called out, pulling her into the circle. The group burst into cheers as the music thumped louder, the bass vibrating through the soles of their feet. Neon lights danced across their faces, painting them in shades of blue and pink. Noma laughed as someone handed her a cup, her worries melting away with each beat of the music.

"I can totally handle this," she thought, sipping the fruity concoction in her hand. Her confidence soared as she twirled under the lights, her sequins catching and reflecting the glow. She was sure she could strike the perfect balance between academics and social life. After all, wasn't this what university was all about—finding yourself, making friends, and enjoying every moment?

But as the night wore on, a niggling thought began to creep in, one she quickly brushed aside. Her unopened textbooks sat untouched on her desk, their crisp pages an unspoken challenge. She could almost hear her mother's voice in the back of her mind—*"Don't forget why you're here, Noma."* But the music drowned out the doubt, and she let the night pull her in once more. *"Tomorrow,"* she promised herself, laughing as the neon lights flickered in her eyes. But deep down, a small voice whispered: *What if tomorrow comes too late?*

Subtle Foreshadowing

Yet, even as she laughed and danced, the faintest shadow lingered in her mind. *"Remember why you're here, Noma."* Her mother's voice once again cut through the music, unwanted but persistent. She exhaled sharply, drowning it in bass and laughter.

The group erupted into a chant, and someone grabbed her hand, pulling her into a spur-of-the-moment dance-off. The crowd cheered as Noma spun around, her cheeks flushed from the effort. This was her moment, her chance to bask in the joy of newfound independence. But beneath the surface, the weight of unfulfilled responsibilities lurked, ready to tip the scales.

The Academic Slide

The first missed lecture felt harmless. The third felt normal. The fifth felt inevitable. After all, she could always catch up later, right? But then one missed class turned into two. Then five. Before she knew it, she was showing up only when absolutely necessary, relying on friends' notes and rushed cramming sessions to stay afloat.

Her once diligent study habits crumbled under the weight of her social life. The books piled up on her desk, unopened. The assignments remained half-done, postponed until the last minute. Every day, she promised herself that she would start fresh—tomorrow. But tomorrow always turned into another distraction.

Even when she wasn't physically out with friends, her phone was a portal to endless distractions. She would sit down to study, only to mindlessly scroll through social media. One notification led to another. A viral challenge on TikTok. A long-winded group chat about an upcoming event. An Instagram post from someone bragging about how much fun they were having.

"I'll just check for a second," she would tell herself. Then, an hour would disappear.

At night, she would lie in bed, the glow of her phone screen illuminating her face, replaying moments from the day, promising herself that she would do better tomorrow. Yet, every morning, the cycle continued.

The Warning Signs

The consequences of her choices crept in slowly, almost unnoticeably at first. Every morning felt like a battle. The alarm would blare, but exhaustion pinned her down. Even when she managed to drag herself out of bed, a fog of fatigue clouded her mind. Sleep deprivation became a normal part of her routine. She constantly felt behind, overwhelmed by the sheer amount of work she had ignored.

Her grades were the first to take the hit. She had always been a top student, but now, test scores came back with red marks slashed across the pages. Essays were returned with comments scribbled in the margins—'rushed,' 'lack of clarity,' 'below standard.'

Her relationships with her professors became strained. One day, as she rushed into class ten minutes late, she tried to quietly slip into her seat. But her professor noticed.

Noma had always been a strong student, but for the first time, she felt like she was slipping through the cracks. No one was reminding her to show up for lectures. No one was checking if she submitted her assignments. It was all on her. And with every skipped class and rushed deadline, the weight of responsibility grew heavier.

When the lecture ended, she approached the desk hesitantly. The professor sighed, flipping through a stack of papers before glancing up.

"I see potential in you," he said, his tone softer than she expected.

"But potential means nothing if you don't put in the effort. You need to start showing up—not just in class, but in your own life."

His words hit hard. She nodded, but her heart pounded. Was it already too late to fix things?

The Breaking Point: Falling Behind and Facing the Consequences

Noma barely noticed how far she had fallen behind—until it was too late.

At first, it was just missing a few lectures, ignoring a couple of readings, and assuming she could catch up later. But as the semester progressed, the gaps in her knowledge became harder to ignore. Deadlines blurred together, and assignments piled up faster than she could manage. She would sit at her desk, pen in hand, but the words wouldn't come. The more she avoided the work, the heavier the weight of failure grew.

Then came the test results.

Her fingers trembled as she clicked on the portal. The red **"Fail"** glared back at her like a wound torn open. A lump formed in her throat. This wasn't a hard test. This was her future slipping away. It wasn't just one test. It wasn't just one class. It was a pattern, a slow unraveling of everything she had worked for.

Still, she told herself she could turn it around. She just needed to focus. She'd **start tomorrow.**

Tomorrow turned into next week. Next week became next month.

And then, reality hit her in the harshest way possible.

The final grades were released.

As she scrolled through the portal, her breath caught in her throat. She had **failed two courses**—including one of her major subjects. There was no retake. No extra credit. No quick fix.

She would have to **repeat the courses next year.**

Her chest tightened. Her friends would **move on**, registering for new modules, progressing toward their degrees, and planning for the future. And she would be stuck—left behind because of her own choices.

Noma had assumed she could juggle everything—fun, freedom, and academics. But now, she saw the truth. She had lost control. She had let distractions dictate her path.

For the first time, she felt the full impact of her decisions.

That night, she sat in the silence of her Residence, staring at the blinking cursor on a blank document. A party invite flashed on her phone. She turned it face down.

For the first time, she ignored it.

The Cost of Change

Noma thought the decision to **fix her mistakes** would be simple. She assumed people would **understand** why she was pulling back from late nights and endless distractions.

She was wrong.

"You're different these days," Thando remarked, tilting her head curiously. "You don't hang out as much."

Noma hesitated. "I know, Thando. I just... I really need to focus right now."

"Focus?" Thando's lips curled slightly, but there was something else in her tone—hurt, maybe?

"So, what, we're just distractions to you?"

The words stung. She wanted to explain that she wasn't rejecting their friendship—she was just trying to fix what she had neglected. But Thando just shook her head, forcing a laugh.

"Do your thing, I guess," she muttered before walking off.

Thando's words echoed in Noma's mind long after she had walked away. A knot formed in her stomach—was choosing to change the same as choosing loneliness?

But not everyone reacted the same way.

A few days later, Lunga slid into the seat next to her in the library. "Hey, I saw you killed it in class today," he said, flashing a grin. "I mean, who would have thought you actually knew stuff?"

Noma rolled her eyes but couldn't help but smile.

"Honestly," Lunga continued, "it's good to see you back at it. We all make mistakes, but seeing you bounce back? That's inspiring."

She exhaled slowly, warmth spreading in her chest.

Noma smiled, the heaviness lifting just a little. Maybe growth wasn't about losing people. Maybe it was about choosing herself—and seeing who stayed.

Interactive Element:

Survey Insight:

"I thought I had everything under control—until I had to retake two courses while my friends moved on. That moment taught me a painful truth: distractions don't feel like distractions until you see the cost."

Reflection Prompt:

- Have you ever underestimated how distractions impact your long-term goals?
- What strategies can you implement to stay focused while still enjoying social life?

The Role of Technology in Distraction & Burnout

Noma's phone was no longer just a tool—it was her escape, her comfort, her constant companion. Mornings began with her thumb swiping before her eyes had fully opened. Nights ended with the screen's glow casting shadows on her pillow.

At first, it started with just casual scrolling—checking Instagram between classes and watching TikTok videos before bed. But soon, she found herself trapped in an endless loop of content. A 5-minute break turned into an hour of mindless scrolling. A simple notification led to an entire evening wasted on viral challenges, campus gossip pages, and influencer posts.

It wasn't just about entertainment—it was a distraction from everything she was avoiding.

Whenever she felt overwhelmed by assignments or upcoming tests, she reached for her phone instead of her books or seeking help. It was easier to lose herself in social media than face the reality of how much work she had left undone.

One night, as she opened her laptop to study, a notification from a group chat popped up.

"Anyone up for a movie night?"

Without thinking, she picked up her phone, replying with a quick *"Maybe."* But instead of getting back to work, she tapped into her favorite influencer's livestream. *Just five minutes*, she told herself. But soon, the video autoplay into another. Then another.

By the time she checked the clock, two hours had disappeared.

Her assignments? Unfinished.

Her textbook? Gathering dust.

Her mind? Stuffed with content—yet when she tried to focus, all she could grasp was a hollow sense of confusion.

Burnout Sets In

The more she tried to juggle her phone and studying, the harder it was to focus.

She noticed the signs but ignored them.

Sleep deprivation due to staying up late watching videos, then waking up groggy, unable to concentrate.

Her attention was short — she struggled to read even two paragraphs before switching to another app.

Feeling guilty about wasted time but repeating the cycle anyway led to feelings of anxiety & stress.

One morning, after only three hours of sleep and rushing to class, she realized she had no idea what the lecture was about. The professor's words drowned in a sea of confusion. Her body was there, but her mind wasn't.

The Breaking Point: When Social Media Took Over

The final straw came during an important group project.

Her teammates had assigned her a key section to research. But the night before the deadline, she got lost in social media again.

Her plan was simple—finish her section, then reward herself with a little TikTok time. But the moment she grabbed her phone, her brain craved the dopamine hit. One video turned into another. Then another.

Before she knew it, the sun was rising.

Her heart pounded as she stared at the empty document. *I'll start now. I still have time.*

But her thoughts were jumbled, her brain fogged from exhaustion. Desperation took over. She copied. Pasted. Tweaked a few words.

It was a mess, and she knew it.

By the time she walked into class, shame clung to her like a second skin. Her teammates' eyes burned into her, their disappointment louder than words.

"You didn't even try," one of them muttered.

Noma swallowed hard, but no excuse could undo what had already been done.

She wanted to defend herself—to explain that she had meant to do it, that she got distracted, that she was just tired. But deep down, she knew the truth.

She had let her phone control her.

That night, Noma sat in her residence room, staring at her screen. For the first time, she didn't feel entertained or connected. She felt exhausted. Defeated. Trapped.

She had always assumed social media was a harmless escape. But now, she realized—it had become her prison.

Interactive Element:

Survey Insight:

"I used to think I could handle social media and studying at the same time. But when I failed my midterms, I realized I had spent more time scrolling than actually reading my textbooks."

Reflection Prompt:

- How much time do you actually spend on your phone each day?

- What habits can you change to create a healthier balance between digital entertainment and productivity?

- How can you use technology to enhance your studies?

The Turning Point: Noma's Wake-Up Call

Noma sat motionless, bathed in the faint glow of her desk lamp. The textbook lay open before her, its words twisting into meaningless scribbles. She blinked. Once. Twice. But the sentences refused to sink in. Her phone sat face-down, but it may as well have been buzzing in her veins. The silence wasn't enough to erase its presence. She didn't need a notification—her fingers twitched toward it anyway, itching for the easy escape.

But tonight was different. Tonight, she felt empty.

She had always told herself she could handle it all—parties, social media, academics—but her slipping grades, strained friendships, and now, the reality of **repeating a major course and extending her studies by an additional year** told a different story.

Her sister's voice echoed in her mind, low but sharp. *"Noma, I expected better from you."*

Her teammates' words cut even deeper. *"You didn't even try."*

She squeezed her eyes shut, but the accusations didn't fade because they were right.

For the first time, she allowed herself to fully acknowledge what she had been avoiding. She wasn't just failing academically—she was losing control in every aspect of her life.

She had let distractions dictate her actions.

And now, she had a choice—keep spiraling or take back control.

Rebuilding from the Ground Up

The next morning, Noma woke up with a clear decision in mind—she was going to fix this.

Noma grabbed a notebook and wrote three words at the top of the page: *Take back control.*

This wasn't just about fixing her grades—it was about breaking free. From distractions. From bad habits. From the version of herself that had let everything spiral.

Her plan had to be real. Concrete.

Step 1: Digital Detox & Time Management

TikTok? Gone. Instagram? Logged out. She couldn't risk falling into the same cycle again.

She set screen time limits on her phone for social apps and kept it out of reach while studying.

Mornings were no longer for scrolling. Instead, she would start her day with ten minutes of focused revision.

Noma was doing well—better than she had in months. Her study schedule was locked in, her focus was sharper, and she was finally catching up on missed material.

Then, one night, she made a simple mistake.

She sat down at her desk, intending to read through her notes. But when she picked up her phone to check a "quick" email, a notification popped up.

A trending post. A viral challenge. A long-forgotten group chat buzzing with activity.

"I'll just check for a second," she told herself.

One post led to another. Ten minutes turned into twenty. Then forty.

When she finally looked up, the clock glared back at her.

12:47 AM.

Her heart sank.

The highlighter in her hand remained idle. The notes are unread. Another night wasted.

She exhaled, pressing her fingers against her temples. *Not again*

How had she let this happen again?

For a moment, she felt like a failure, like all her progress had been erased. But then she shook her head.

No. One mistake doesn't undo everything.

She turned off her phone, pushed it far away, and refocused.

She wouldn't let one slip define her. This wasn't about being perfect—it was about learning, adapting, and getting back up.

Step 2: Rebuilding Academics

She met with a student advisor to find ways to catch up on what she had missed. To avoid last-minute panic sessions, she mapped out a structured study plan—studying in small, daily sessions instead of cramming the night before. She also committed to attending lectures regularly and found ways to stay engaged in class discussions.

Step 3: Accountability & Support System

Noma joined a study group, surrounding herself with learners who wanted to succeed.

She apologized to her group project teammates and asked for a second chance to prove she was serious.

She sought mentorship from Ms. Dlamini, who agreed to guide her through this rebuilding phase.

The Downfall of a Semester: Repeating a Module and Delaying Graduation

The First Small Wins

The first week was tough. Breaking bad habits wasn't easy. Some nights, the urge to pick up her phone was almost unbearable. And there were times she felt overwhelmed by how much she had fallen behind.

But then, the first small victories started happening.

- She completed an assignment on time—a first in weeks.
- She raised her hand in class to answer a question—and got it right.
- She felt focused for the first time in months.

With every small win, her confidence grew.

Key Takeaways from This Chapter

Freedom Requires Self-Discipline – College and university offer more independence than high school, but without proper time management, it's easy to fall behind academically.

Small Distractions Have Big Consequences – Spending too much time on social media or socializing can cause missed deadlines, lower grades, and more stress.

Failing a Course is a Setback, Not the End – Struggling academically is normal, but it's a chance to rethink your priorities and develop better habits.

Not Everyone Will Support Your Growth – Making positive changes may cause you to lose some friendships, but it is essential to surround yourself with people who encourage success.

Rebuilding Takes Time, but it's Possible – By sticking to a study routine, asking for help when needed, and staying focused, you can get back on track and make real progress.

Noma realized something: **Discipline wasn't about punishing yourself—it was about taking control of your own future.**

Interactive Element:

Survey Insight:

"I used to believe that 'fixing my habits' would take forever, but once I started, I realized that even small changes made a huge difference. One focused study session led to two. Then three. Then, a new routine. It's possible."

Reflection Prompt:

- What is one small habit you can change today that will improve your focus and productivity and change the direction of your life?

- How can you hold yourself accountable for making this change while still enjoying your academic journey and maintaining a balanced social life?

For so long, she had let distractions control her, mistaking endless scrolling and impulsive decisions for "living in the moment." But she saw the truth now: Freedom without responsibility led to setbacks. And setbacks? They weren't failures. They were lessons.

With every small step—attending lectures, studying with focus, surrounding herself with people who uplifted her—she was rebuilding the future she nearly lost.

For the first time in a long time, she wasn't drowning in distractions. She was present, aware, and in control.

She glanced at her phone; a party invitation blinked on her screen.

This time, she didn't hesitate.

She put her phone down, turned back to her notes, and smiled.

Motivational Quote:

"Discipline is not about punishment—it's about taking control of your future. The choices you make today shape the life you live tomorrow."

Chapter 3:

Campus Safety 101 - What Every Student Should Know

The Safe Haven?

Lebo checked the time on her phone—8:45 PM.

The warm glow of the campus library had faded behind her as she stepped onto the pavement. The night air wrapped around her in an unsettling chill, and though the path ahead was familiar, tonight, it felt different.

Her fingers curled around her backpack straps, gripping them tighter with every step. *Fifteen minutes. Well-lit paths. Safe.* That's what she kept telling herself. But the words felt hollow like a whisper lost in a storm.

Something felt off.

She picked up her pace, her sneakers scuffing the pavement. Then—a faint shuffle. Close. Too close. *An echo? No. Someone.* The space between each step tightened, mirroring hers. Matching. Following.

There was another set.

Close.

Too close.

Her heart pounded as she forced herself to remain calm. *Maybe it's just another student walking home.*

But the footsteps stayed in sync with hers. Every turn, every quickened step —matched.

She gripped her phone tightly, her mind racing. Her sister's voice rang in her head:

"If you ever feel unsafe, trust your gut. Get to a crowded area. Stay alert."

She heard laughter ahead – students leaving late. Finally, a chance. She slowed down, took a deep breath, and slipped into their group like she belonged there. She stole a quick glance over her shoulder—the figure paused, then turned away.

From the corner of her eye, she saw the shadow of a man stop briefly and then walk away in the opposite direction.

Lebo swallowed hard. *Maybe he was harmless. Maybe it was just her imagination.*

But what if it wasn't?

She let out a shaky breath.

The campus is supposed to be a safe space. But safety isn't always guaranteed.

Interactive Element: Trusting Your Instincts

Survey Insight:

"I always thought I was just being paranoid when I felt unsafe walking alone at night. But when I ignored my gut feeling once, I ended up in a dangerous situation. Trusting your instincts isn't paranoia—it's protection."

- Have you ever felt unsafe in a familiar environment? What did you do?

- What small precautions can you take to ensure your safety when traveling alone at night?

When Campus Safety Feels Like a Myth

For many students, college and university represent newfound **freedom, growth, and opportunity**—a place to explore independence and chase ambitions. Campuses are often seen as safe spaces designed for learning and community. But beneath this sense of security lies an unsettling reality: crime is an ever-present risk. From **muggings and theft** to more serious threats like **gender-based violence (GBV) and drink spiking**, students must be aware of their surroundings and take precautions.

The question is—how do you navigate campus life **without living in constant fear**?

While colleges and universities are meant to be secure environments, crime is a reality on many campuses.

For Lebo, the campus had been a shield—a world where danger belonged elsewhere. Until Nthabiseng came home one night, shoulders hunched, her breath unsteady. "What happened?" Lebo whispered.

Nthabiseng's fingers trembled. "I don't want to talk about it."

At that moment, Lebo realized just how fragile the sense of security on campus truly was.

The Harsh Reality: A Campus Incident

Nthabiseng sat on the edge of her bed, her hands shaking as she tried to speak.

"I was walking back from the library," she whispered, her voice unsteady. "At first, I thought I was just overthinking. But then—when I stopped, he stopped. When I crossed the street, so did he. Step for step. Watching. Waiting."

A chill ran down Lebo's spine. She knew that feeling all too well—the creeping unease, the sharp awareness of every shadow. She had walked alone at night before, heart pounding, convinced someone was behind her. And now, hearing Nthabiseng's fear, that same dread settled deep in her chest.

Nthabiseng exhaled shakily, her breath uneven. "I ran into the student center just in time," she said, swallowing hard. "He just… stopped outside. Didn't move. Just stood there. Watching."

A long silence settled between them.

The campus had security guards, surveillance cameras, and well-lit pathways—but none of it guaranteed safety.

This wasn't paranoia. This was real.

Campus Crime in South Africa: What the Numbers Say

Campus crime isn't just one person's bad experience—it's a national issue.

Theft & Muggings: A 2023 study on South African college and university campuses revealed that 40% of students had experienced or witnessed phone or laptop theft. Many incidents occur near public transport stops, shortcuts, or empty pathways.

Gender-Based Violence (GBV): In a 2022 student safety survey, over 30% of female students reported experiencing some form of harassment or assault near campus premises.

Drink Spiking & Substance-Related Risks: Bars and social spaces near colleges and universities are hotspots for spiked drinks and drug-related crimes. Many don't realize their drink has been spiked **until they wake up unable to remember what happened.**

These aren't just numbers—they reflect the real dangers faced by students daily.

Why Are Students at Risk?

False Sense of Security: Many students assume campuses are safe from crime, so they let their guard down in familiar places.

Walking Alone at Night – Late study sessions, campus events, or long travel times often leave students walking home alone. **Many areas are poorly lit, and security patrols aren't always reliable.**

Distractions: Earphones, phones, or social media scrolling make students less aware of their surroundings.

Lack of Reporting: Many incidents go unreported because students assume nothing can be done or feel shame about speaking up.

Interactive Element: Breaking the Silence

Survey Insight:

"I never thought I'd be a victim of crime at university—until it happened to me. The scariest part wasn't the incident itself, but the fact that I felt alone after it happened."

Reflection Prompt:

- **What are the barriers stopping students from reporting crimes?** (Fear? Stigma? Lack of action?)

- What steps can colleges and universities take to improve student safety and encourage crime reporting?

Prevention Strategies: Staying Safe on Campus

Knowing the risks is only the first step. The real power lies in prevention—taking active steps to protect yourself and create a culture of safety on campus.

For Lebo, Nthabiseng's close call was a reminder of the reality she had already faced, but it drove the point home with a clarity she hadn't fully grasped until then.

That night, after hearing Nthabiseng's story, she opened her laptop and started researching.

How do students protect themselves on campus?

What she found was eye-opening.

Personal Safety Habits

Stay Alert

Your phone can wait! That quick text or song change isn't worth the risk. Keep your head up and **be aware of your surroundings**, especially at night.

Walk in Groups When Possible

Walking with friends isn't just more fun—it's safer. **Avoid walking home alone at night, let someone know your route and estimated time of arrival – but your phone should stay in your pocket or bag.**

Use Safe Paths & Well-Lit Areas

Stick to designated pedestrian paths and avoid shortcuts through secluded spaces.

Trust your Gut

If something feels off, take action. Walk toward a crowded area, enter a public space, or call emergency services.

Keep Emergency Contacts Ready

Your university's security hotline and local emergency contacts should be saved on your phone.

Lebo realized that small habits can make a big difference.

Digital Safety & Online Awareness

In today's world, threats aren't just physical. Online safety is just as important.

Avoid Sharing Your Location in Real Time

Posting your **location in real-time** may seem harmless—until someone you don't know starts tracking your movements. **Delay your posts or keep locations private.**

Be Careful with Personal Information like your PIN code

Never share your **student ID, home address, or banking details** over **email, text messages, or social media platforms.**

Beware of Scams & Fraudulent Messages

Colleges and universities will never ask for **your passwords, banking details, or personal identification numbers (PINs)** via email. If a message seems suspicious—**STOP. VERIFY. REPORT.**

Watch for Online Harassment & Stalking

If someone **won't stop messaging you, shares your pictures without permission, or threatens you**, don't ignore it. **Block them, report them, and seek support.** Cyberstalking is a crime.

Lebo never realized how vulnerable students were online—until she started paying closer attention.

Campus Resources & Reporting Incidents

One of the biggest barriers to safety is silence. Many students don't report incidents because they:

- Feel like they're "overreacting"

- Assume nothing will be done

- Fear of being blamed or judged

But speaking up matters.

Know Where to Report

Every university or **Technical Vocational Education and Training (TVET) college** has a safety office, student support services, or a campus security hotline. Find out where yours is **now**—so you don't have to search when it's urgent.

Use Safe Transport Services

Many colleges and universities offer **shuttle services or escorted walks home** at night. Check what your **campus provides**—and **use it.**

Get Involved in Safety Initiatives

Safety isn't just the responsibility of your college or university —it's **a student movement.** Join or support **student-led initiatives** that work with campus security.

Encourage Friends to Speak Up

Many students **stay silent after experiencing crime**. If a friend is struggling, **listen, support, and encourage them to report.**

As Lebo read through these prevention tips, she felt empowered for the first time.

She couldn't control the world. But she could control how she moved through it.

Interactive Element: Taking Action

Survey Insight:

"I used to think safety was just about luck, but now I know that small actions—like walking with friends and staying aware—can prevent incidents."

Reflection Prompt:

- What are three safety habits you can start practicing today?
- How can students encourage a culture of safety on campus?

"Building a Safer Campus Together"

Campuses are safer when students stay informed and take action. Most universities and colleges have **security policies, but they only work if students know how to use them and stay alert.**

That realization hit Lebo as she listened to learners sharing safety concerns at a student forum.

- "Campus lighting is too dim in some areas—why hasn't it been fixed?"
- "Security-only shows up after something happens. We need more patrols."
- "People don't report crimes because they feel like nothing will change."

As the discussion continued, she realized the power students had.

Students Who Advocate for Change:

Your voice matters. Student councils have successfully pushed for **better security policies, increased patrols, and safer campus design** - but only when students speak up.

Change starts with a conversation. Many college and university **safety boards** respond to student concerns, which can lead to real policy changes. Reporting isn't complaining—it's building a safer future.

Action leads to results. Student-led campaigns have driven the **installation of panic buttons, improved street lighting, and safer shuttle services**. What could your campus change?

Lebo's friend Lunga leaned over and whispered, "We should actually do something about this."

She nodded. It was definitely time to take action.

Interactive Element: Creating a Culture of Safety

Survey Insight:

"When students engage with campus safety initiatives, meaningful improvements happen. Awareness and active participation help create a safer environment for everyone."

Reflection Prompt:

- What safety improvements would you suggest for your university?

- How can you encourage more conversations about student security?

Public Transport and Off-Campus Safety

Campus safety doesn't stop at the gates. For many students, getting to and from campus comes with its own set of risks.

Lebo had always loved the freedom of city life. University meant exploring new places, meeting new people, and moving beyond the limits of her hometown.

But that freedom came with responsibility.

One evening, after a late study session, Lebo found herself waiting at an unfamiliar bus stop.

The dim streetlight flickered, casting long shadows. A few strangers stood nearby—too quiet, too still.

She tightened her grip on her bag, scanning the street for a sign of the bus. A sound—footsteps behind her. Slow. Measured.

Her heartbeat quickened.

Was she imagining it? Or was someone watching her?

The minutes dragged. She checked her phone—1% battery.

Finally, headlights pierced the darkness. As the bus pulled up, relief crashed over her like a wave. She climbed in quickly, choosing a seat near the driver.

That night, Lebo made a decision—she wouldn't wait until something happened to start taking safety seriously, not after everything she's been through and the lessons she'd learned.

Practical Tips for Public Transport Safety:

- **Plan Your Routes Ahead**: Use reliable apps like Moovit or Google Maps to plan your journeys in advance so you don't have to worry about getting lost or stuck in a sketchy area. These apps are super useful to making sure you're taking the safest route, especially when you're out late. They can help you find well-lit streets, avoid areas that feel off, and even show you if there are any delays or changes in your public transport schedule.

- **Stay in Well-Lit Areas**: Always wait for transport in brightly lit, crowded places.

- **Share Your Location**: Use safety apps like Life360 or Namola to share your real-time location with family or trusted friends. Both apps mentioned are useful for safety, but they serve different purposes. Life360 is great for staying connected with family, tracking each other's locations and ensuring everyone's safe. Namola is designed for emergencies, helping you quickly get in touch with emergency services if something is wrong.

- **Be Alert**: Avoid distractions like headphones or phones when waiting or walking, especially in unfamiliar areas.

Collaboration for Safer Commutes: At first, the complaints about safety felt like background noise—something students vented about but never acted on. But then, small actions started making a difference. A student-led safety committee started petitions urging the university to improve campus lighting. Meetings with local authorities led to increased police patrols near public transport areas. The most effective change, however, was the buddy system—students teaming up for late-night walks, making what was once a lonely and risky journey home safer.

Interactive Element: What steps can you take to ensure your safety during travel? List three practical actions you can adopt today.

Cybersecurity and Digital Safety

But safety isn't just about physical threats. In today's digital age, risks can follow you beyond campus—right into your inbox, social media, and financial accounts. Students often overlook online security, but cyber threats can be just as damaging as real-world dangers.

In today's world, campus safety isn't just about physical spaces—it's about online spaces, too. Many students assume that cybersecurity is only a concern for professionals or businesses, but in reality, college and university students are prime targets for cyber threats, scams, and digital harassment.

Lebo learned this the hard way.

She barely glanced at the email before clicking. The red **URGENT: ACCOUNT VERIFICATION REQUIRED** subject line sent a jolt of anxiety through her—what if she got locked out of the student portal? She skimmed the message. The university logo was right there. The tone was formal, almost robotic. Her fingers hesitated over the keyboard for a moment, a flicker of doubt passing through her mind. But the fear of missing an important deadline outweighed the hesitation. She typed in her details and pressed enter. The page refreshed. Nothing seemed off.

At first, it was just an inconvenience—her university portal refused to log her in. She reset her password, annoyed but not alarmed. Then, an email arrived about a transaction she didn't recognize. Her stomach tightened. More alerts followed. By the time she reached the Student Finance Office, dread had fully settled in.

The administrator gave her a fleeting look before nodding knowingly.

"You're not the first," he sighed. "It was a phishing scam."

The words hit like a cold wave. She had walked straight into a trap.

Other students had fallen for similar scams, losing access to financial aid portals, email accounts, and even personal bank information.

The more she researched, the more she realized how unprotected most students were online.

Common Cybersecurity Threats for Students

Phishing Scams – Fake emails pretending to be from colleges, universities, banks, or scholarship providers to steal login details.

Identity Theft – Using personal information for fraudulent activities, including SIM-swap fraud.

Social media Oversharing – Posting location details or personal schedules that expose students to real-world risks.

Cyberbullying and Online Harassment – Deliberate attacks or abusive behavior on social media or anonymous platforms that can harm mental health.

Protecting Yourself Online

Use Strong Passwords & Two-Factor Authentication

Avoid using the same password for multiple accounts. Use password managers and enable 2FA wherever possible.

Verify Before You Click

If you receive an email asking for login or personal details, verify the sender first. Colleges and universities don't ask for sensitive data via email.

Keep Your Social Media Private

Adjust your privacy settings to control who sees your posts. Avoid sharing real-time location or personal schedules.

Report Cyber Harassment Immediately

If you're experiencing online stalking, cyberbullying, or threats, report them to campus IT, law enforcement, or platforms like Take Back the Tech. Take Back the Tech is a global movement that encourages people, especially women and girls, to use technology in ways that fight back against online abuse and violence. It's about taking control of our devices and digital spaces to protect ourselves and promote safety online. This campaign helps spread awareness about the risks of cyberbullying and offers ways to take action against it by using technology as a tool for good.

Interactive Element: Securing Your Digital Life

Survey Insight:

"I didn't take online safety seriously until my student account got hacked. Now, I double-check every email, and I never share personal details publicly."

Reflection Prompt:

- What steps can you take today to enhance your digital security?
- Have you ever encountered an online scam or cyber threat? How did you handle it?

Real safety isn't about living in fear—it's about knowledge, preparation, and the power of looking out for one another.

Creating a Culture of Safety

Through their own experiences, Lebo and Nthabiseng came to realize that while personal safety is important, real change happens when students unite to build a culture of safety.

Being safe on campus isn't just about avoiding risks; it's about creating an environment where everyone looks out for each other.

At first, the complaints about dimly lit pathways were just that—complaints. Students grumbled, but nothing changed. Then, a few voices turned into a petition. The petition turned into meetings with university officials. What started as frustration became a movement, and months later, new floodlights illuminated the once-dark walkways. As Lebo stood beneath them one evening, she realized something powerful: safety wasn't just about avoiding danger—it was about demanding better systems, better support, and a culture that prioritizes student well-being.

That's when she realized—safety is a shared responsibility.

How Students Can Create a Safer Campus

Report Safety Concerns Promptly

Many students hesitate to report suspicious activity, but reporting things early can help prevent bigger problems.

Advocate for Safety Improvements

Student bodies can work with college or university leadership to enhance security measures, improve transport systems, and increase digital safety awareness.

or Support Safety Committees

Many campuses have peer-led safety programs that organize awareness drives, self-defense workshops, and emergency training.

Support Survivors & Encourage Open Conversations

Creating safe spaces for students to share their experiences without judgment reduces the stigma around reporting incidents.

Lebo's student group launched "Campus Safety Week," where experts held discussions on gender-based violence prevention, digital security, and public transport safety. The response was overwhelming - students were eager to learn how to protect themselves and each other.

She realized that one voice can spark a conversation, but it takes many voices to drive change.

Interactive Element: How Can You Make a Difference?

Survey Insight:

"I always thought safety was just about self-defense, but I've realized that real safety comes from supporting each other and demanding change together."

Reflection Prompt:

- What safety initiative or improvement could you introduce at your college or university?

- How can you encourage more conversations about student safety on your campus?

Resources and Support Systems

A strong campus safety culture isn't just about awareness—it's also about having access to the right resources and support systems when needed.

Lebo had become more cautious in her daily routine, but one night, she overheard a friend say, *"Even if something happened to me, I wouldn't know where to go for help."*

That struck her.

It wasn't just about avoiding danger—it was about knowing where to turn when danger found you. She realized that most students, herself included, didn't always know how to report an incident, where to get emergency assistance, or how to find support after a traumatic experience. That had to change.

This section provides an overview of essential resources every student should be aware of.

University and Colleges Safety Services

Campus Security & Emergency Contacts

Every university has a campus security office—but students often don't know the emergency numbers by heart.

Tip: Save these numbers in your phone and keep a printed copy in your wallet.

Safe Walk Programs & Student Escort Services

Many universities and colleges offer on-demand safety escort services at night—this helps students get home safely without walking alone.

Mental Health & Trauma Support Centers

Experiencing a safety-related incident can have lasting emotional effects. Colleges and universities often have counselors and trauma support specialists available to help students recover.

Safety Apps & Digital Tools

In today's world, safety isn't just about physical security—it's also about digital awareness.

Namola – South Africa's leading **emergency response app,** connects users to police, medical teams, and roadside assistance.

Use apps like **Life360 or WhatsApp Live Location** to share your real-time location with trusted friends or family members.

Google Personal Safety App & Emergency SOS – Allows you to activate emergency alerts, share your location, and check in with contacts during emergencies.

Most smartphones come with **built-in emergency features**—go to your settings and **set up your Emergency SOS button today** to quickly call for help when needed.

Tip: Enable location tracking only for trusted people—avoid oversharing movements on public platforms.

External Support Systems & Legal Aid

South African Police Service (SAPS) Student Desk

Works with colleges and universities to address crime affecting students, including theft, assault, and fraud.

Legal Aid South Africa

If you ever face a legal challenge related to your safety, don't navigate it alone. Free and affordable legal support is available for students.

NGOs Fighting Gender-Based Violence (GBV)

Organizations like **Tears Foundation & Thuthuzela Care Centres (available nationwide)** provide free support, counseling, and legal aid for survivors.

Tip: If you or someone you know is in crisis, reach out to peer support groups—you are never alone.

Interactive Element: Do You Know Your Safety Resources?

Survey Insight:

"I didn't know half of these resources existed until I needed them. Universities should make this information more accessible for all students."

Reflection Prompt:

- Have you saved your college or university's emergency contacts on your phone?

- What safety apps or tools can you start using today?

Reflections and Takeaways

As Lebo and Nthabiseng sat in the student lounge, they couldn't help reflecting on how much their perspectives had shifted.

At the start of university, they had believed safety was something automatic—something they didn't need to think about. But after real experiences, tough conversations, and seeing the power of student advocacy, they had learned an important truth:

- Safety is not just about avoiding danger—it's about awareness, preparation, and collective responsibility.

- Being proactive instead of reactive is the key to reducing risks.

- A strong campus safety culture benefits everyone.

More than anything, they realized that safety isn't just a personal concern—it's a shared commitment. When students support each other, advocate for better security, and educate themselves about risks, real change happens.

Key Takeaways from This Chapter

- **Be aware of your surroundings** – Never assume that familiar spaces are always safe.

- **Trust your instincts** – If something feels wrong, take action immediately.

- **Use resources and support systems** – Know your campus security services, legal aid options, and digital safety tools.

- **Look out for others** – A safer campus is created when students take collective responsibility for each other.

- **Speak up and take action** – Report safety concerns, join safety advocacy groups, and push for necessary changes.

Interactive Element: Gratitude and Self-Reflection

Survey Insight:

"I used to take safety for granted, but after a close call, I realized how much I appreciate the small habits that protect me every day."

Reflection Prompt:

- What is one safety habit or resource you are most grateful for?

- How can you help others feel safer in your community?

Final Closing: Empowerment through Awareness

It's easy for students to assume safety is someone else's responsibility. But real safety begins with awareness, action, and collective empowerment.

By understanding risks, preparing for challenges, and looking out for one another, awareness turns into real protection.

Remember:

Safety begins with awareness and grows through action.

A safer campus is not necessarily a perfect one—it's one where people actively look out for each other.

Noma and Lebo knew they couldn't control every risk. But what they could do—what every student could do—was take ownership of their safety and the safety of their community.

That small shift in mindset is where real empowerment starts.

What's Next?

What's one step you can take today to be more aware and proactive about your safety?

Motivational Quote:

"Safety isn't just about avoiding risks—it's about being prepared, aware, and looking out for one another. A safer campus begins with you."

Chapter 4:

Did You Check on Me?

WHAT TO DO IF YOU FAILED GRADE 12

Turning Failure into Hope: The Role of Community in Preventing Suicide

"I felt like my whole future had been taken away from me," Nolubabalo recalls. "I didn't know what to do or where to turn."

The release of her Grade 12 results shattered Nolubabalo's world. Despite years of hard work and dreaming of becoming a pharmacist, her results felt like a failure. The pressure of her ambition, combined with the weight of expectations from her family and community, weighed heavily on her.

"I felt like I had let everyone down - my family, my friends, myself," she confesses. "I didn't see a way out, and for a moment, I thought ending my life was the only solution."

Her first instinct was to hide her pain, to mask her emotions with a brave face, pretending everything was okay. But the crushing sense of disappointment and shame followed her everywhere, especially when walking through the streets of her village.

It wasn't until she turned to her grandmother, the one person who had always been her anchor, that Nolubabalo found the courage to confront her feelings. Talking to her grandmother helped her realize that she wasn't alone in her struggle – and that it was okay to seek help, even in her darkest moments.

In moments like these, it can feel as if the world is closing in but community is often where healing begins. A kind word from a neighbour, a supportive teacher, or a listening ear from family can make all the difference. Sometimes, it takes just one person believing in you to help you believe in yourself again.

"Oh *mntana we ntombi yam,* allow yourself to grieve. It's okay to feel sad and disappointed. But don't let those feelings consume you. You are more than your failure."

Nolubabalo's story is not unique. Most learners who fail - especially in communities where education is seen as the only path out of poverty - struggle with intense feelings of shame, guilt, and hopelessness.

The pressure to succeed can be overwhelming. For some, it feels like their worth is tied entirely to academic performance. The fear of judgment, disappointment, and rejection becomes paralyzing, leaving little room to process failure in a healthy way.

But failure doesn't have to be the end of the road.

With the right support, learners like Nolubabalo can begin to see that their lives still have meaning and possibility – even after disappointment. Family, educators, and the broader community play a crucial role in helping young people feel seen, supported, and guided toward their next steps.

It starts with reminding them *their worth is not defined by one exam.*

Next Steps to Move Forward:

• **Explore Rewrite Opportunities:** Many schools and community centers offer Grade 12 rewrite programs, giving you another chance to improve your marks.

• **Look into Bridging Courses:** Universities and TVET colleges often have foundation programs to help you meet entry requirements.

- **Seek Career Guidance:** Career centers and local NGOs can help you explore other pathways in health, business, or vocational training.

- **Reach Out for Emotional Support:** Speak to a counselor, trusted teacher, or support line to help you process your feelings in a healthy way.

Failing Isn't the End: A Roadmap to Recovery and Renewal

Step 1: Acknowledge Your Emotions and Break the Silence

Failure can trigger intense feelings – shame, guilt, sadness, and even fear. These emotions are valid. What makes them harder to carry is the silence and stigma surrounding them. By naming what you're feeling and opening up to someone you trust, you begin the process of healing. Talking about failure helps break the cycle of isolation and creates a more supportive, non-judgmental environment where growth becomes possible.

Step 2: Reassess Your Goals and Aspirations

After opening up to her grandmother, Nolubabalo started reflecting honestly on her journey. She revisited her dreams – not just the surface-level goal of becoming a pharmacist, but the deeper desire to help her community. This shift in perspective helped her reconnect with her *why*.

She began to explore alternative paths – vocational training, apprenticeships, and online courses that aligned with her purpose. Eventually, she discovered a two-year healthcare vocational program that would equip her with the skills to make a meaningful impact, even if the route looked different from what she originally envisioned.

Step 3: Foster a Growth Mindset

We need to move away from a mindset that equates success with self-worth and instead embrace one that values effort, learning, and perseverance. A growth mindset helps learners understand that failure isn't the end – it's a stepping stone.

When learners are taught to see setbacks as opportunities to learn and grow, they begin to develop resilience. They realize that their abilities can be developed through hard work and dedication and that one moment of failure doesn't define their future.

Step 4: Focus on Your Strengths

While parents and caregivers may have their own hopes for your future, it's important that learners respectfully express their own goals and passions. Self-advocacy is part of growing into your identity.

Take time to reflect on what you're good at - your skills, positive traits, and past accomplishments. Shifting your focus from what went wrong to what you bring to the table can rebuild confidence. Celebrate your wins no matter how small they may seem. They are building blocks for your next chapter.

Step 5: Encourage Help-Seeking Behavior

It's vital to create safe and supportive environments where learners feel seen, heard, and empowered to ask for help. Too often, fear of judgment or appearing "weak" keeps young people silent in their pain.

Nolubabalo realized she couldn't carry the weight of her struggles alone. Reaching out for support - from her grandmother, mentors, and eventually counselors – was the turning point in her journey. Seeking help isn't a sign of weakness; it's a powerful step toward healing and moving forward.

Step 6: Support and Resources

Support can make all the difference between giving up and starting over. When Nolubabalo reached out to her career guidance teacher, it opened up new pathways. She also discovered local NGOs and community centers offering mentorship, emotional support and job training.

Learners who fail need access to tangible resources - counseling, vocational training, mentorship programs, and safe spaces to process their emotions. With the right guidance and tools, moving forward becomes possible.

Step 7: Stay Committed and Persevere

With renewed purpose, Nolubabalo took action. She enrolled in the vocational training program, fully committed to her studies, and determined to rebuild her future. Along the way, she leaned on the support of family, friends, her church, and her own resilience.

It wasn't always easy - there were moments of doubt and exhaustion – but she kept going.

Two years later, Nolubabalo graduated, equipped with the skills and confidence to make a difference in the healthcare sector. Her journey proved that failure is not the end – it can be the beginning of a new path paved with courage, growth, and perseverance.

"I'm not the same person I was two years ago," Nolubabalo says with a quiet smile.

"I'm stronger, more resilient, and more determined. I know that I can overcome any obstacle – as long as I have the right mindset and a strong support system."

The Silent Struggle

Thando sat in the canteen, staring blankly at the cup of tea in front of her. The steam had long faded, leaving behind a lifeless puddle of brown liquid. Her plate of food was untouched, a silent reminder of yet another meal she had no energy to eat.

The world around her was alive. Laughter erupted from one table. A heated debate about football carried on at another. The clinking of plates and scraping of cutlery filled the room.

It was as if she were trapped behind a soundproof glass wall. Watching, hearing, existing, but never truly present.

No one could see how empty she felt inside.

She ran her fingers absent-mindedly along the rim of the cup, her mind drowning in thoughts too heavy to carry. She couldn't pinpoint when it had begun - this exhaustion that was more than just tiredness. It was bone-deep, relentless, pressing against her chest from the moment she opened her eyes. Even breathing felt like work, as though every inhale required permission from an unseen force.

She moved through the day like she was walking through thick fog, barely connected to her own life.

She showed up to class even though she could hardly absorb a word. She laughed at her friends' jokes, even though the sound felt foreign, leaving her lips. She posted smiling selfies, even though she hated the reflection staring back at her.

To everyone else, she was fine.

To herself, she was disappearing.

The Mask of Pretending

"Are you okay?"

The words stopped Thando in her tracks.

They came from Nomvula, a classmate she barely spoke to, as they crossed paths outside the lecture hall.

For a split second, Thando froze. Had her mask slipped?

She forced a smile, the kind she had perfected. The kind that made her look put together, even when she was falling apart.

"Yeah, just tired," she said quickly.

"Too many assignments, you know?"

Nomvula nodded knowingly. "Tell me about it! I can't wait for this semester to end."

And just like that, the conversation was over. Nomvula walked away, satisfied with the answer.

Because that's what people did.

They asked, but they didn't really want the truth. They saw, but only what was easy to believe. They heard, but only the words that reassured them.

Not many looked deeper.

And so, Thando kept pretending.

A Song That Spoke the Words She Couldn't Say

That night, Thando lay in bed, the glow of her phone screen illuminating the darkness around her. She wasn't reading messages or checking emails - just scrolling mindlessly, trying to silence the thoughts in her head.

Then, a familiar song played in the background.

Libianca's People.

I've been drinking more alcohol for the past for the past five days

"Did you check on me? Now, did you look for me?"

"I walked in the room, eyes red, and I don't smoke banga."

"Did you check on me?"

"Now, did you notice me?"

"Nobody will know the paranoia, oh."

"Cause I put a smile on my face, a façade you can never face (hoo)."

"And if you don't know me well, well, oh."

"You won't see how buried I am inside my grave, inside my grave."

"Cause you see people, people, people, people. "

"They don't really know, they don't really know you."

As she listened to the lyrics, something inside her cracked.

"I walked in the room, eyes red, and I don't smoke banga..."

She wasn't drinking. She wasn't smoking. But the feeling was the same.

A lump rose in her throat.

"Did you check on me? Did you look for me?"

The words cut deep.

Had anyone? Had anyone truly seen past her tired smile, past her, I'm okay?

She curled onto her side, gripping the blanket like an anchor, as if holding onto something physical could keep her from slipping further into the emptiness.

For the first time in weeks, she allowed herself to feel the weight she had been carrying.

She had become an expert at pretending. But beneath the mask, all she wanted was for someone to see her - really see her.

Warm tears slipped past her closed eyelids.

No one had really checked on her. Not in the way that mattered. Not in the way that asked past the automatic "I'm fine."

Not just a passing "How are you?"

Not just a casual "You good?"

But someone who truly meant it. Someone who would notice the unspoken signs - the hesitation before answering, the forced smile, the way her voice sounded too light for someone carrying so much.

Someone who wouldn't move on so easily.

The Hidden Reality of Mental Health in College and University Life

At first glance, college and university life appears vibrant and full of promise. Lecture halls buzzing with conversations, late-night study sessions, and friendships forming in crowded canteens. But beneath the surface, an unspoken battle rages - one that many students fight alone.

For students like Thando, the weight of expectations, academic pressure, and personal struggles wasn't just overwhelming - it was suffocating.

Mental health struggles in institutions of higher learning are not just about stress - they are also about survival.

For countless students, every day is a quiet battle, fought in silence because speaking up seems like admitting defeat.

The pressure to perform academically while dealing with internal battles leaves students emotionally drained.

Social isolation and the stigma surrounding mental health make it difficult for students to reach out for help.

The normalization of suffering in silence leads many to believe they are alone in their pain.

Despite being surrounded by thousands of students, many feel completely alone.

Thando wasn't just dealing with stress - she was sinking.

She had spent months pretending. Showing up for class, engaging in conversations, and even posting happy photos online. But inside, she felt like she was disappearing.

The reality of mental health struggles in college and university is raw and often overlooked. Suicide, anxiety, and depression are not rare occurrences - they are part of the lived experiences of numerous students who feel unheard and unseen.

Yet, institutions rarely talk about it in ways that matter.

Interactive Element: Have You Checked on Someone Today?

Survey Insight:

"I thought my friends were fine because they laughed, showed up, and kept going. But when I finally shared my struggles, I realized how many of them had been silently drowning too."

Reflection Prompt:

- Think about a time you were struggling. Did anyone check on you? How did that feel?

- Who in your life might need you to check on them today?

Understanding Mental Health Challenges

For many students, mental health struggles don't announce themselves loudly. They creep in silently - through exhaustion that never goes away, feelings of isolation in a crowded room, or the crushing pressure to succeed.

Thando's experience was not unique. Millions of students around the world suffer in silence, afraid to speak up because they don't want to be seen as weak.

But the reality is - mental health struggles are real, and they affect each person differently.

The Most Common Mental Health Struggles among Students

Childhood Traumas

Anxiety & Panic Disorders

Your heart pounds before exams, your mind races at night, and no matter how much you prepare, the fear of failing never fades. Excessive worry, restlessness, difficulty concentrating, and overwhelming fear of failure become a constant presence in your life. These feelings don't just vanish after the test or event. They follow you, seeping into your daily routine.

For example, you might feel physically sick before an exam or avoid social situations altogether due to anxiety. It's not just the stress of a big event; it's the constant tension in your body, the mental exhaustion of trying to quiet your mind, and the emotional toll it takes on your self-esteem and relationships. You may find it harder to connect with others, as you feel like you're carrying an invisible weight that others can't see. Anxiety doesn't just affect what you do; it affects how you see yourself and how you interact with the world.

Depression & Persistent Sadness

The things you once loved feel meaningless, sleep offers no escape, and even small tasks drain you. You smile so no one asks questions, but it's exhausting. Depression isn't just about feeling sad – it's a heaviness that lingers, a fog that doesn't lift. You may lose interest in hobbies, struggle to get out of bed, or feel emotionally numb. It's the weight of everything and nothing, all at once.

Common Signs:

- Loss of interest in activities you once enjoyed
- Constant fatigue, sleeping too much or too little
- Difficulty concentrating or making decisions
- Feelings of worthlessness

- Changes in appetite

- Emotional numbness or feeling "disconnected" from life

Example: Skipping lectures, ignoring messages from friends, or crying for no clear reason. Feeling like the future holds nothing to look forward to – and like you're too tired to care.

Burnout & Academic Pressure

You're constantly working, but it never feels like enough. You push through exhaustion, hoping the next deadline will bring relief – but it doesn't. Burnout creeps in slowly: first, you're just tired. Then, you're emotionally numb, disconnected from what you once cared about. Academic pressure can turn learning into a survival mode, where joy and motivation disappear.

Common Signs:

- Constant exhaustion, even after rest

- Feeling detached or indifferent toward schoolwork

- Decline in academic performance despite effort

- Irritability, brain fog, or forgetfulness

- No longer enjoying hobbies or social time

- Feeling like you're on autopilot

Example: Pulling all-nighters but not retaining anything. Going through the motions at college or university while secretly wondering if you're falling apart.

Suicidal Thoughts & Self-Harm

It's more than just sadness – it's a deep sense of hopelessness. You might feel like life has no purpose, start pulling away from people you care about, or begin hurting yourself to cope.

Common Signs

- Talking about death or disappearing

- Giving away meaningful items

- Ignoring friends and family

- Showing sudden changes in mood

Example: Not replying to messages for days, saying things like "I won't be around much longer," or harming yourself when the emotional pain feels too heavy.

The Silent Struggles Students Face

Many students struggling with their mental health stay silent - not because they don't want help, but because they feel they can't. The fear of being judged, pressure to meet expectations, and the exhausting act of pretending everything is okay often keep them quiet.

Fear of Judgment & Stigma – *"What if they think I'm weak?"*

Many students stay silent – not out of apathy but because they fear being misunderstood or dismissed. In a world that often equates struggle with weakness, asking for help can feel like risking your dignity.

Cultural & Family Expectations – In some families, mental health isn't discussed – it's denied, dismissed, or spiritualized. Struggles are minimized as "just stress" or seen as weakness, not illness. The pressure to uphold family honor, be strong, or just "pray it away" can make it even harder to speak up. For many, seeking help feels like betraying cultural values or disappointing loved ones.

Social Media Pressure – Everyone else seems happy, successful, and thriving. But behind the filters and perfect captions, no one posts the sleepless nights, the silent breakdowns, or the moments of self-doubt. Comparing real-life struggles to the highlight reels on Instagram and TikTok can leave students feeling inadequate, isolated, and like they're falling behind in a race no one really understands.

Lack of Awareness – Many students don't recognize the signs of deteriorating mental health until they hit a breaking point. They might brush off feelings of exhaustion, irritability, or sadness as just part of the college or university experience, thinking it's normal to feel overwhelmed. However, these signs can easily go unnoticed until they become too overwhelming to ignore, making it even harder to seek help when it's most needed.

Thando didn't even realize how bad things had gotten for her.

She thought she was just tired.

She thought she just needed to push through.

She thought everyone else was handling things better than her.

But in reality? She needed help.

And she wasn't alone.

Interactive Element: Recognizing the Signs

Survey Insight:

"I didn't realize I was struggling with depression until someone pointed out that I had stopped laughing, stopped caring, and started isolating myself."

Reflection Prompt:

- Have you noticed changes in your own behavior or mood that might be warning signs?

- Think about your friends—have you noticed any red flags in someone close to you?

Recognizing the Signs

Just because someone says they're fine doesn't mean they are.

Most people struggling with mental health don't vocalize it - they show small, subtle signs through changes in behavior, mood, or habits that are easy to overlook.

The real challenge? Recognizing these signs before it's too late.

Warning Signs in Yourself

Have you ever felt "off" but couldn't explain why?

Mental health struggles can sneak up on you - often before *you* even notice. Sometimes, the signs aren't loud. Sometimes, they aren't obvious - even to ourselves.

You're always exhausted, even after resting.

"No matter how much I sleep, I wake up tired and unmotivated."

You don't enjoy the things you used to.

"I used to love hanging out with my friends, but now I just cancel plans."

You feel overwhelmed all the time.

"I don't know how to handle everything - I feel like I'm constantly behind."

You're withdrawing from people.

"I ignore texts, I don't return calls, and I just want to be left alone."

You experience random mood swings.

"Some days, I feel okay. Other days, I don't even recognize myself."

If you're experiencing several of these signs, it's important to check in with yourself and seek support.

Warning Signs in a Friend or Classmate

People rarely say, "*I'm not okay.*" Instead, they show it.

Sudden changes in personality

A usually social person becomes withdrawn.

Constant fatigue or loss of motivation

They stop engaging in class or group projects.

Avoiding social activities

They cancel plans frequently or stop responding altogether.

Joking about feeling hopeless

They make dark jokes about life being meaningless.

Extreme mood changes

They are either too hyper or too detached.

Changes in appearance or hygiene

They stop taking care of themselves.

What To Do If You Notice These Signs

Don't wait until they ask for help.

Many people suffer in silence because they don't want to "burden" others.

Ask open-ended questions.

Instead of "*Are you okay?*" (which is easy to dismiss), try:

"I've noticed you seem different lately. Want to talk?"

"I'm here for you, no judgment. How have you been feeling?

Check in regularly.

One conversation isn't enough. Keep checking in. Even a simple "*Thinking of you*" message can mean a lot.

Encourage them to seek help.

Offer to go with them to a counseling session or help them find a support group.

Interactive Element: Who Do You Need to Check On?

Survey Insight:

"*I assumed my friend was fine because they still showed up to class. I wish I had checked on them sooner.*"

Reflection Prompt:

- Think of three people in your life - have any of them seemed different lately?
- How can you reach out to them today in a way that shows you care?

Building Resilience

Recognizing the signs of mental health struggles is important - but just as important is learning how to cope, heal, and strengthen your emotional resilience.

Resilience doesn't mean having it all together.

It's not about avoiding the pain of difficulty – it's about learning to adapt, recover, and keep going - even when things feel heavy. It's the quiet strength that helps you move forward, one step at a time.

Thando wasn't sure how to fix everything she was feeling, but she knew she needed to start somewhere.

Understanding Resilience: What It Is (And What It Isn't)

Resilience IS:

- Learning how to handle stress and bounce back after setbacks.
- Building healthy habits that strengthen mental and emotional well-being.

- Seeking support when needed - not struggling alone.

Resilience is NOT:

- Pretending everything is fine when it's not.

- Ignoring emotions and bottling up pain.

- Believing you have to do everything alone.

Thando realized resilience wasn't about "being strong." It was about allowing herself to heal, set boundaries, and take small steps forward - at her own pace. She recognized that resilience wasn't about being "strong" all the time but about giving herself the grace to heal and space to grow.

Practical Ways to Strengthen your Mental Resilience

1. Prioritize Rest & Self-Care

Your mind and body are not machines. Make time to rest, recharge, and do things that nourish you – whether that's sleep, a hobby, or simply breathing space.

Thando started setting a consistent bedtime and unplugging from social media before bed.

2. Tackle Big Challenges in Smaller Steps

When everything feels overwhelming, break it down. Focusing on one task at a time can help you feel more in control.

When assignments piled up, she stopped panicking and created a simple plan - one task at a time.

3. Stay Connected to your Support System

Talk to someone you trust. You don't have to carry everything alone. Sometimes, just being heard makes a big difference.

Thando realized she didn't have to handle everything alone. Checking in with friends made her feel lighter, not weaker. Instead of shutting everyone out - she started reaching out whenever she needed help.

4. Set and Protect Healthy Boundaries

It's okay to say no. Your energy is valuable – don't pour from an empty cup.

Saying no to plans didn't mean Thando was boring - it meant she valued her well-being. Protecting her peace was an act of self-respect. She learned to say no when she was overwhelmed.

5. Practice Gratitude & Self-Affirmation

It may feel small, but reminding yourself of your worth and noticing what's good – even briefly – can slowly shift how you see yourself and your world.

Every night, she wrote three small things she was grateful for, shifting her focus from stress to appreciation.

6. Practice Self-Compassion

Don't beat yourself up for not being okay. Speak to yourself the way you would to a friend – with patience, kindness, and care.

The Power of Talking to Someone

At first, Thando wasn't sure if talking to someone would help.

But one day, she finally opened up to a counselor.

"I thought they would just give me generic advice, but they really listened. I didn't feel like I was being judged. For the first time, I felt understood."

Seeking help doesn't mean something is wrong with you - it means you care enough about yourself to heal.

Interactive Element: What Are Your Resilience Habits?

Survey Insight:

"I used to think resilience meant dealing with everything on my own. Now I know it means asking for help when I need it."

Reflection Prompt:

- What's one practical step you can take today to strengthen your emotional resilience?

- What helps you recharge when life feels overwhelming?

Resources & Support Systems

One of the biggest barriers to mental health recovery isn't always the struggle itself - it's not knowing where to turn for help.

Thando had spent months believing she had to figure things out on her own. But when she finally reached out, she was surprised by how much support was available - both on campus and beyond.

Whether it's counseling services, peer support groups, helplines, or online communities, help is out there. Students just need to know where to look – and that it's okay to ask.

University and College Mental Health Services

Counseling Centers & Therapy Sessions

Most universities and colleges provide on-campus counseling services - offering free or low-cost therapy for students facing stress, anxiety, or depression.

Tip: Check your student portal or campus wellness office for details on booking an appointment.

Support Groups & Peer Counseling

Many campuses have peer-led mental health support groups where students can connect and talk openly with others who understand their struggles.

Crisis Hotlines & Emergency Support

Some universities and colleges provide 24/7 mental health crisis support, offering a direct helpline for students in immediate distress.

External Mental Health Support (South African Context)

SADAG (South African Depression & Anxiety Group)

Helpline: 0800 567 567

Provides free crisis intervention, suicide prevention, and counseling referrals.

Lifeline South Africa

Helpline: 0861 322 322

Supports individuals facing emotional distress, GBV trauma, self-harm crises, and mental health challenges.

Tears Foundation (GBV & Trauma Support)

Helpline: 010 590 5920

Offers legal assistance, trauma counseling, and survivor support for gender-based violence.

Digital Mental Health Resources

Mindfulness & Therapy Apps

Headspace & Calm – Guided meditation and stress relief techniques.

BetterHelp & Talkspace – Online therapy platforms offering accessible virtual counseling for students.

AI Mental Health Chatbots & Support

Wysa – AI-driven emotional support chatbot, helpful for managing daily stress and anxiety.

Community Support Platforms

7 Cups – Peer-led anonymous online support groups for students struggling with loneliness, anxiety, and depression.

Encouraging a Culture of Seeking Help

One of the biggest myths about mental health support is:

"If I ask for help, I'm weak."

But the reality is that asking for help is a sign of strength, not weakness.

Many students struggle in silence because they think their problems aren't "serious enough" for therapy or support groups. But mental wellness isn't about how bad things are - it's about taking care of yourself before they get worse.

Where to Find Help

If you or someone you know is feeling hopeless or thinking about ending their life, please reach out for help.

- South African Depression and Anxiety Group (SADAG) Suicide Helpline: 0800 567 567

- Lifeline South Africa: 0861 322 322

  Your life matters, and there is always someone ready to listen.

Interactive Element: Do You Know Where to Find Help?

Survey Insight:

"I had no idea my university offered free therapy until a friend mentioned it. More students need to know about these resources."

- Have you ever saved a mental health helpline or support contact on your phone – just in case you or someone you care about ever needs it?

- What's one mental wellness app or service you can start using today?

Reflections & Takeaways

Thando never imagined that a simple song lyric - "*Did you check on me?*" - would be the moment she realized just how much she needed someone to care enough to ask.

Now she knew – she wasn't the only one carrying this kind of pain.

Everyone carries silent struggles at some point.

Some wear them on their faces.

Others hide them behind smiles and *"I'm fine."*

And many are simply waiting for someone to notice.

Key Takeaways from This Chapter

Mental health struggles aren't always visible, and they can affect anyone.

Checking in on others, even with a simple "How are you?" can make a life-changing difference.

Building resilience involves small, consistent actions – and not isolating yourself.

Seeking help isn't a sign of weakness - it's a courageous step toward healing.

A strong support system, whether friends, therapy, or community resources, is crucial for emotional well-being.

Normalizing conversations around mental health creates a safe space for healing and connection.

Thando didn't have all the answers. She was still figuring things out. But for the first time in a long while, she didn't feel alone. She started reaching out to friends - not just when she needed help, but also to check on them.

She saved emergency helplines on her phone.

She committed to prioritizing her mental health the same way she had always prioritized her academics.

And with that, she realized - healing doesn't happen all at once, but every small step counts.

Interactive Element: Gratitude & Self-Reflection

Survey Insight:

"*I used to keep everything bottled up until I learned that vulnerability isn't weakness - it's how we heal.*"

Reflection Prompt:

- What's one thing you're grateful for when it comes to your mental well-being?

- Who's one person you can check in on this week to remind them they're not alone?

Remember, mental well-being is a journey, not a destination. Every small step, no matter how quiet or subtle, moves you closer to healing. And by checking in on others, you help create a support system that can carry us all forward.

Motivational Quote:

"*Healing doesn't happen all at once, but every small step matters. Checking in on yourself and others can change everything.*"

"You may encounter many defeats, but you must not be defeated."

Maya Angelou

Chapter 5:

Binaries & Boxes (LGBTQI+)

Brotherly Love and Betrayal

Mzi never imagined the worst heartbreak of his life would come from his own family.

He'd prepared himself for awkward questions from distant relatives. He'd even expected judgment from conservative elders in the community. But he never saw it coming - that Themba, his own brother, would be the one to betray him.

It happened on a normal Sunday afternoon.

Mzi and Themba were sitting on the front steps of their home, laughing over an inside joke about their childhood. For a moment, everything felt usual—like it always had.

Then, without thinking, Mzi said it.

"There's something I need to tell you."

Themba chuckled. "You sound serious, bro. What's up?"

Mzi's hands clenched into fists. He had played this moment over and over in his head for years. Maybe he shouldn't say anything. Maybe it would ruin everything.

But he was tired of hiding.

"I'm gay."

The laughter stopped.

Themba's expression shifted so fast that Mzi barely recognized him. His eyes hardened, his jaw clenched, and at that moment, Mzi felt everything between them shatter.

"You're joking, right?" Themba's voice was hollow.

Mzi swallowed hard. "No."

For a long moment, silence filled the space between them. Then, Themba stood up and walked away.

He didn't look back.

The Loneliness of Rejection

The days that followed were a blur of silence and avoidance.

Themba stopped talking to him. He no longer invited Mzi to their usual weekend hangouts. At home, it felt like Mzi had become a stranger.

The rejection burned deeper than anything he had ever felt before.

Mzi had heard stories—of families turning their backs, of doors closing forever. Of people losing everything just for being honest.

He never thought he'd be one of them.

For the first time, he wondered—had he made a mistake by telling the truth?

He isn't alone in this struggle. Across South Africa, approximately 60% of first graders ultimately drop out before completing 12th grade. While comprehensive national statistics on LGBTQ+ student dropout rates are limited, countless stories echo Mzi's —young people leaving school not due to academic challenges but because of constant stigma and discrimination.

Mzi thought about those students—about how many had sat in their rooms, just like he was now, questioning if they had made a mistake by being themselves. It sank in slowly – heavy, unshakeable.

But then, something unexpected happened.

The Power of Reconciliation

Weeks passed before Themba finally spoke to him again.

It was late in the evening when Mzi walked into the kitchen to find his brother standing there, staring at the kettle as it boiled.

"I don't get it,"

Themba finally said, his voice quieter than usual.

Mzi hesitated. "What?"

"You. I don't get how you... became this way."

Mzi sighed. He had prepared himself for arguments, for anger, for more silence—but he hadn't expected this.

"Themba," he said, his voice steady, "I didn't 'become' anything. This is who I've always been."

His brother looked at him then—really looked at him. For the first time since that day on the steps, Mzi saw something in Themba's eyes that wasn't a disappointment.

"I don't understand it," Themba admitted. "But I don't want to lose you."

Mzi had spent weeks grieving a brother who was still alive. And now, here he was—making an effort.

Not promising, not pretending to understand, but trying.

It wasn't perfect. It wasn't easy.

But it was a start.

Family Dynamics and Cultural Expectations

For many LGBTQI+ individuals, the family often extends beyond blood—it's about finding identity, belonging, and survival in spaces where acceptance may not be guaranteed. In cultures where traditional gender roles and expectations around sexuality are deeply rooted, coming out isn't just a personal choice—it's a challenge to the very fabric of culture.

Mzi had always known that being gay wasn't just taboo—it was the kind of truth families buried in silence.

His parents avoided the topic. His uncles laughed about "fixing" boys who weren't masculine enough. His church warned against "corrupt influences."

So where did that leave him?

The Weight of Cultural Expectations

"Our Family Name Comes First"

In many communities, especially in African and religiously conservative households, honor and family reputation come before individuality.

Mzi had heard it a hundred times:

- "What will the neighbors say?"

- "Your choices don't just affect you. They affect all of us."

- "We didn't raise you like this."

Traditional Masculinity & Femininity

Many cultures still cling to rigid gender roles – where strength is expected of men and obedience of women.

Queerness is often viewed as a "betrayal of traditional values."

Religious & Social Pressures

Many LGBTQI+ individuals face spiritual rejection, with some being told they need to be "healed" or "prayed over."

Religious texts are often misinterpreted to justify exclusion and discrimination.

For Mzi, the fear of losing his family had kept him silent for years.

How do you choose between honesty and belonging? Between being yourself and being loved?

For many, it's not a choice—it's survival.

When Love is Conditional

Mzi never wanted to believe that love could be conditional.

But when he came out, he realized something painful—love, for some, came with terms and conditions.

"We love you, but don't talk about it in front of the family."

"You can live your life, but don't bring your partner home."

"We still care about you, but you're different now."

It wasn't the kind of rejection that came with yelling or slammed doors.
It came in the pauses before a response, the way conversations shifted when he entered a room, the quiet reminders that love—at least in his family—had limits.

Finding Chosen Family

For LGBTQI+ individuals, "family" isn't always about blood—it's about love, acceptance, and community.

Mzi learned that sometimes, your real family isn't the one you're born into—it's the one you build.

He found family in:

- Friends who loved him exactly as he was.
- Queer support groups that made him feel seen.
- Online communities that reminded him he wasn't alone.

Interactive Element: Navigating Family Expectations

Survey Insight:

"I thought coming out would bring me closer to my family, but instead, it made me realize who truly loved me unconditionally."

Reflection Prompt:

- How has your family's cultural background shaped your views on identity and self-expression?
- Have you ever had to hide a part of yourself to be accepted? How did that feel?

Navigating Campus Life as an LGBTQI+ Student

For many students, college or university is a place of self-discovery and newfound freedom.

But for LGBTQI+ students, it can also be a space filled with contradictions—where openness is encouraged, yet discrimination still lingers in unexpected places.

For Mzi, moving to campus meant he could finally breathe.

At home, he was always careful—lowering his voice, adjusting his mannerisms, hiding parts of himself to avoid confrontation.

But here?

- There were LGBTQI+ student groups.

- People openly discussed gender identity and sexuality without shame.

- There were professors and classmates who embraced diversity.

For the first time, Mzi felt like he belonged.

But that didn't mean life on campus was always safe.

Microaggressions & Everyday Discrimination

Not all discrimination is loud. Sometimes, it's in the quiet way people treat you differently.

"You don't look gay."

As if queerness comes with a dress code.

"I don't have a problem with LGBTQI+ people, but do you have to talk about it so much?"

But straight people talk about their relationships all the time.

"We can be friends, just don't hit on me."

Because every queer person is automatically attracted to them?

Jokes that aren't really jokes.

The constant side comments, the *"it's just a joke, don't be so sensitive."* The whispers behind backs.

Mzi learned to laugh it off. But over time, the small things added up.

They made him second-guess himself.

They made him adjust his personality in certain spaces.

They made him wonder if he was truly accepted—or just tolerated.

Visibility without Safety

Being "out" doesn't mean being safe.

Not all LGBTQI+ students have the privilege of being open about their identity.

Mzi had friends who:

Used fake names on queer dating apps to avoid being outed.

Chose not to hold hands with their partners in public.

Hesitated before correcting someone who misgendered them.

Even on a so-called progressive campus, safety wasn't a given. Hate crimes weren't just statistics.

Queerphobia wasn't just online—it was in classrooms, in their Residence, in the way some professors skipped over LGBTQI+ topics like they didn't exist.

Mzi learned that existing in queer spaces on campus came with risks—but also with power.

Finding Safe Spaces on Campus

LGBTQI+ Student Organizations & Pride Clubs

More than just a group—these spaces become lifelines. Here, students find support, share experiences, and push for real change.

Campus Counseling & LGBTQI+ Mental Health Resources

Safe, non-judgmental spaces for students struggling with identity, discrimination, or family rejection.

Supportive Professors & Faculty Allies

Finding faculty members who actively support LGBTQI+ inclusion made a difference.

Online & Anonymous LGBTQI+ Communities

When the real world didn't feel safe, online queer spaces became a lifeline – places of comfort, connection and belonging.

For Mzi, joining an LGBTQI+ student group was the turning point. For the first time, he was surrounded by people who understood—truly understood.

People who didn't just accept him but celebrated him.

Interactive Element: Creating Inclusive Campus Spaces

Survey Insight:

"Being queer on campus is easier than in my hometown, but it's still exhausting having to explain why I deserve respect."

Reflection Prompt:

- If your campus is supportive, what makes it feel safe?

- If your campus is NOT inclusive, what changes would make it better?

The Trauma of Rejection

For many LGBTQI+ individuals, rejection isn't just a moment—it's a lasting wound that shapes how they see themselves and navigate the world.

Mzi had always known that coming out would be difficult. He had prepared for shock, discomfort, and even awkward silences.

But he hadn't prepared for the pain of being treated differently by the very people who once claimed to love him unconditionally. If love had conditions all along, was it ever truly unconditional?

The Emotional & Psychological Impact of Rejection

Rejection doesn't always come in obvious ways. Sometimes, it's subtle but just as painful.

Being excluded by friends and family from gatherings.

Suddenly, there are no more invitations to "boys' nights" or "family prayer meetings."

Conversations that used to be warm now feel forced.

"So… when are you bringing home a girlfriend?"

Backhanded acceptance.

"I still love you, but I don't support your lifestyle."

Being seen as a "phase" instead of a person.

"You'll grow out of it."

"This is just a Western thing—our culture doesn't allow this."

Threats and ultimatums.

"If you keep this up, you're on your own."

"You can't live here anymore."

Religious manipulation.

"Pray the gay away."

"God didn't make you this way."

Mzi had heard variations of all these reactions—from family, community members, and even strangers who had no right to an opinion on his life.

Little by little, it became harder to breathe under the weight of it all.

Mental Health Consequences of Rejection

Anxiety & Hypervigilance

Living in fear of judgment can lead to anxiety and hypervigilance.

Imagine never being able to fully relax. You're always watching, always bracing for something to go wrong – even when nothing's happening. That's what hypervigilance feels like.

Depression & Self-Doubt

Rejection doesn't just hurt at the moment – it can plant seeds of self-doubt that grow quietly over time. For many, it leads to questioning their worth, wondering if they'll ever be accepted for who they are. That kind of emotional weight can feed into depression, making it hard to find joy, motivation, or even the strength to hope.

Internalized Homophobia

Many battle internalized homophobia— the quiet voice that whispers, *"Maybe they're right. Maybe something is wrong with me."* It's what happens when the prejudice around you starts to shape how you see yourself. You begin to absorb other people's hate, turning it inward until it feels like truth.

Loneliness & Isolation

This isn't just about feeling alone; it's about feeling invisible or misunderstood. The fear of rejection keeps them from truly connecting with others, even when they're surrounded by people. Without support, a person can feel isolated in a world that doesn't always accept them for who they are. It's a constant struggle of pretending to fit in while feeling like an outsider.

Isolation isn't just about missing out on social moments – it's about feeling like you can't fully be yourself anywhere.

Increased Suicide Risk

Studies show that LGBTQI+ youth are at significantly higher risk of suicide due to family rejection and social exclusion.

Mzi never thought he would experience the kind of sadness that makes you question your existence.

But after weeks of silence from his family, he began to wonder if life would always feel this lonely.

He wasn't alone.

So many LGBTQI+ individuals have walked this road. Some made it out stronger.

Others didn't make it at all.

Healing from Rejection: Rebuilding Self-Worth

One day, Mzi stumbled upon an online forum for queer South Africans.

For the first time, he saw his own pain reflected in the words of others.

"It's not your job to convince people to love you. The right people will."

"Your existence is not a mistake. You are not broken."

"You deserve to take up space exactly as you are."

Something shifted inside him.

Healing from rejection isn't about "getting over it"—it's about learning that your worth isn't defined by who accepts you.

Mzi started focusing on things that made him feel alive again.

- Therapy & LGBTQI+ support groups.
- Writing letters to himself, reminding himself that he mattered.

- Spending time with friends who made him feel seen.

- Learning to separate his identity from other people's expectations.

The pain didn't disappear overnight. But slowly, he started believing in himself again.

Interactive Element: Healing & Moving Forward

Survey Insight:

"I used to think I had to earn love by changing myself. But now I know—real love doesn't ask you to shrink."

Reflection Prompt:

- Have you ever faced rejection for simply being yourself? How did it affect you?

- What's one act of self-love you can do today to remind yourself that you are enough?

The Role of Allies & Building Inclusive Spaces

For LGBTQI+ individuals, having allies isn't just about support—it's about survival.

An ally is someone who doesn't just say they accept LGBTQI+ people but also takes real steps to make them feel safe and valued. Here's how:

Listening and Learning:

Allies take the time to listen to LGBTQI+ individual's experiences and try to understand what they go through.

Speaking Up:

They call out any hurtful language or behavior they see, whether it's in conversation, at work, or anywhere else.

Sharing the Spotlight:

Allies make sure LGBTQI+ voices are heard, giving them space to speak and be taken seriously.

Taking Action:

Allies support policies that protect LGBTQI+ rights and show up for things like Pride events or LGBTQI+-friendly organizations.

Being There:

They create a safe space for LGBTQI+ people to talk about their struggles without fear or judgment.

Rejection had left its scars. But Mzi also learned that just as words could wound, they could also heal.

That's what true allyship did.

It came from a friend who defended him when someone made a homophobic joke.

It came from the professor who included LGBTQI+ perspectives in classroom discussions.

It came from the stranger who stood beside him at his first Pride event, letting him know he wasn't alone.

Allies make the world safer—one conversation, one action, one stand at a time.

What Does It Mean to Be an Ally?

Listening Without Judgment

Not every conversation needs a debate. Sometimes, the most powerful thing you can say is, "*I hear you.*"

Instead of saying, "*But what about religion/culture?*" say, "*Tell me about your experience.*"

Challenging Homophobia & Transphobia

When people make discriminatory comments, speak up. Silence allows hate to spread. Your voice can make a difference.

Using Inclusive Language & Respecting Pronouns

Instead of assuming someone's gender or pronouns, ask respectfully.

Example: *"What pronouns do you use?"* instead of *"What are you really?"*

Being Visible in Support

Show that you stand with LGBTQI+ individuals, not just in private but in public spaces, too. Share resources, support LGBTQI+ businesses, and celebrate Pride without making it about yourself.

Creating Safer Spaces in Everyday Life

In Schools, Colleges & Universities:

- Recommend gender-neutral bathrooms.

- Support LGBTQI+ student organizations.

- Encourage inclusive policies that protect LGBTQI+ students from discrimination.

In Families & Communities:

- Speak up when family members say harmful things about LGBTQI+ people.

- Help elders with LGBTQI+ experiences through calm, respectful conversations that invite empathy rather than conflict.

- Create spaces where queer family members feel safe to be themselves.

- Report hate speech and bullying.

- Support LGBTQI+ voices all year round, not just when it's trendy or during Pride Month.

- Be mindful of outing someone—never assume it's your place to disclose their identity.

The Power of One Person's Support

Mzi never forgot the day a friend stood up for him in a crowded room. Someone had made a homophobic joke, expecting everyone to laugh. But instead of laughing, his friend turned to them and said:

"That's not funny. You're talking about real people's lives."

It was just one sentence. But in that moment, Mzi felt something he hadn't in a long time—safe.

Because sometimes, the loudest form of allyship is just refusing to stay silent.

Interactive Element: What Kind of Ally Are You?

Survey Insight:

"*I used to think being an ally was just about 'not being homophobic.' But now I know it's about actively standing up for LGBTQI+ people.*"

Reflection Prompt:

- What's one thing you can do to make a space more inclusive for LGBTQI+ people in your life?

- Have you ever stayed silent when you should have spoken up? How would you handle it differently next time?

Support Networks & Resources

Mzi had spent years believing he had to navigate everything alone. But one of the most important lessons he learned was this:

There are people and organizations dedicated to supporting LGBTQI+ individuals. He just had to find them.

When he finally reached out—whether it was to a queer support group, a therapist, or an online community—he realized something powerful:

Help is available. You just have to know where to look.

LGBTQI+ Support Organizations & Helplines

The Triangle Project (South Africa)

Offers mental health support, legal assistance, and HIV prevention services for LGBTQI+ individuals.

Helpline: 021 712 6699

OUT LGBT Well-Being (South Africa)

Provides counseling, sexual health education, and advocacy for LGBTQI+ rights.

Helpline: 012 430 3272

SADAG (South African Depression & Anxiety Group)

For LGBTQI+ individuals facing depression, anxiety, or suicidal thoughts.

24-Hour Helpline: 0800 567 567

Tears Foundation (For GBV & LGBTQI+ Trauma Support)

Assists LGBTQI+ individuals who have faced gender-based violence or hate crimes.

Helpline: 010 590 5920

LGBTQI+ Mental Health & Therapy Resources

BetterHelp & Talkspace (Online Therapy for LGBTQI+ Individuals)

Access queer-friendly therapists from anywhere in the world.

Wysa & MindDoc (Mental Health Apps)

Chat anonymously with AI-based mental health support.

University LGBTQI+ Counseling Services

Many campuses offer safe, affirming therapy sessions for LGBTQI+ students struggling with identity, discrimination, or family rejection.

Peer Support Groups (Both Online & In-Person)

Finding people who share your experiences can be life-changing.

Mzi realized that healing wasn't about forgetting the pain—it was about finding the people who could help carry it.

Legal Protections & LGBTQI+ Rights in South Africa

Legalizing Same-Sex Marriage

South Africa was the first African country to legalize same-sex marriage in 2006.

Protection from Discrimination

The Constitution explicitly protects LGBTQI+ individuals from workplace and housing discrimination.

Reporting Hate Crimes & Discrimination

If an LGBTQI+ person experiences hate speech, discrimination, or violence, they can:

- Report it to SAPS (South African Police Service).
- Seek legal aid from organizations like OUT LGBT Well-Being.

LGBTQI+ individuals fleeing persecution in other countries can apply for asylum in South Africa.

Knowing his rights gave Mzi a sense of power he never had before.

Because knowledge wasn't just about safety—it was about reclaiming his voice.

Interactive Element: Do You Know Where to Find Help?

Survey Insight:

"I thought I was alone until I found an LGBTQI+ support group. It changed everything."

Reflection Prompt:

- Have you saved a mental health helpline or LGBTQI+ resource on your phone in case you or a friend ever need it?

- What's one support network or service you can start using today?

Reflections & Takeaways

Mzi had spent years fearing rejection, questioning his worth, and struggling to find his place.

But through everything—the heartbreak, the healing, the moments of doubt and courage—he had learned one truth:

He was never meant to fit into anyone else's expectations.

He was meant to exist fully, as he was, without apology.

And no one—not his family, not society, not the voices that told him he was "too much" or "not enough"—could take that away from him.

Because he had never been the problem.

And he had always belonged.

Key Takeaways from This Chapter

- Coming out is a deeply personal journey—there's no "right way" or "right time."

- Family doesn't always understand, but chosen family can offer the love and support you need.

- Campus life can be freeing, but it comes with its own challenges—find your safe spaces.

- Rejection is painful, but healing is possible—and you don't have to do it alone.

- Allies play a critical role in making the world safer for LGBTQI+ individuals.

- There are support networks, organizations, and legal protections available.

Mzi realized that self-acceptance wasn't just about surviving—it was about thriving.

It was about standing tall in his truth.

It was about walking with pride, even when the world made it difficult.

It was about knowing that he had always been enough—exactly as he was.

Interactive Element: Your Journey, Your Reflection

Survey Insight:

"I used to think I had to hide who I was to be accepted. Now I know the people who truly love me never ask me to shrink myself."

- What is one part of your identity that you've struggled to accept?

- How can you start showing up for yourself unapologetically?

Final Closing: Celebrating Diversity

If you take one thing from this chapter, let it be this:

You don't have to prove your worth. You don't have to shrink yourself. You are enough, just as you are.

And if the world doesn't give you a space to exist freely, create your own.

Diversity is not a weakness—it is the most beautiful strength we have.

And you deserve to take up space.

Chapter 6:

The Toxic Trio

"A Night to Forget"

Nthabiseng woke up with a pounding headache, her throat dry as sandpaper.

The room was dimly lit, the air thick with a smell she couldn't place. Her body ached in places she didn't understand.

Something felt wrong.

She swallowed hard and tried to sit up, but a wave of nausea hit her, forcing her back down. Her eyes darted around the room. This wasn't her room. A sinking feeling settled in her stomach as she forced herself to scan her surroundings. Clothes were scattered across the floor, a half-empty bottle of something strong on the nightstand. A stranger's belongings… AND, next to her, a body. Still asleep.

Nthabiseng froze. She reached for her phone with trembling hands. **9:47 a.m.**

Flashes of the night before came in fragments. The party. The drinks. The blurry laughter. Someone handing her another shot. Her legs felt heavier than usual. Someone whispering in her ear…and then - nothing.

Nothing!

She squeezed her eyes shut, willing a memory to surface, but all that came was a terrifying blankness. Her pulse quickened as the reality hit her. She didn't remember how she got here. She didn't remember what had happened, but her body knew.

Her body felt violated. Panic surged in her chest.

She looked down at herself. The unfamiliar sheets...The person lying next to her...Her stomach twisted in horror! She had been too out of it to say yes. Too impaired to fight back. Her heartbeat thundered in her ears, drowning everything else out. The weight of the unknown pressed against her chest, heavy and suffocating.

She needed to get out.

She needed to breathe.

She needed to understand what had happened to her.

The Reality of Risky Situations

Nthabiseng's experience wasn't just a rough night out.

It was a harsh truth that far too many students face, where substance use, blurred boundaries, and gender-based violence intersect in ways no one prepares you for.

One moment, it's just a drink. The next, your mind is foggy, your guard is down, and your ability to consent is gone. Then comes the morning after. Waking up in an unfamiliar bed, trying to piece together what happened, and carrying the weight of something you never agreed to!

For Nthabiseng, it started like any other night out, but it ended in confusion, fear, and trauma. And the hardest part? No one prepares you for this. Not at orientation. Not when it matters most.

This chapter unpacks what we call the *Toxic Trio* - the dangerous mix of sexual health risks, substance use, and gender-based violence.

These three issues don't just overlap but feed off each other, creating situations that leave students vulnerable, often with no warning and no one to turn to.

Interactive Element: Recognizing the Risks

Survey Insight:

"I never thought one night of drinking could change my life. But looking back, I wish I had understood the risks better..."

Reflection Prompt:

- Have you ever been in a situation where you felt vulnerable or unsafe - whether due to alcohol, peer pressure, or simply not knowing what was happening around you?

- What practical steps could you take to ensure your safety and that of your friends in social settings?

Sexual Health Awareness

Nthabiseng sat on her bed, scrolling through her phone with a mix of exhaustion and unease.

Her friends dismissed it.

"It was just a mistake. You were drunk. Forget it."

But she couldn't.

What if the gaps in her memory hid something worse?

What if her body now carried a consequence she never chose?

What if silence only made things worse?

No one had ever told her how to handle this. Growing up, sex education, if you could even call it that, was nothing more than whispered warnings:

Stay away from boys.

Good girls don't talk about these things.

If you get pregnant, you're on your own.

But what about everything else? What about consent? Protection? STIs? Emergency contraception? No one had prepared her for any of it. Now, as she sat staring at her phone, scrolling through symptom checkers and crisis hotlines, Nthabiseng realized something painful - Being unprepared wasn't an excuse; it was a trap!

Because when it comes to sexual health, the biggest danger isn't just the risks. It's not knowing how to protect yourself in the first place.

1. The Gaps in Sexual Health Education

Lack of Comprehensive Sex Education

Many students arrive at college or university with more knowledge of fear and shame than of sexual health. While they may have access to information, knowing *how* to apply it in real-life situations is an entirely different challenge.

For some, their only exposure to sex education is abstinence-only messaging, a narrow approach that avoids crucial topics like contraception, sexually transmitted infections (STIs), consent, and bodily autonomy – the right to make informed decisions about your own body without pressure, guilt or being pushed into anything.

Misinformation from Peers & Social Media

Too many students learn about sex from TikTok videos, whispered gossip, or "that one friend who claims to know it all." The result? Harmful myths that sound true but aren't.

For example, believing that "pulling out" is a safe way to prevent pregnancy, when actually it's very risky and doesn't protect against STIs. Or, thinking you can't get pregnant the first time you have sex – a common belief that leaves many unprepared and at risk. Or seeing a viral post that says you can't get pregnant if you drink cooldrink right after sex – a ridiculous myth that's been shared over and over online!

Stigma & Cultural Barriers

In many communities, talking openly about sex, contraception, or anything related to sexual health is considered shameful. These topics are often swept under the rug, framed as "inappropriate" or "not for good girls and boys." As a result, young people grow up in environments where asking questions feels wrong and needing help feels like failure.

The silence has real consequences.

When learners and students experience a scare – whether it's a missed period, a potential STI exposure, or even an experience of assault – they often do not know where to turn. They might be too afraid to go to a clinic or too embarrassed to talk to a parent or teacher. Shame becomes a barrier to safety.

Example: Khanya, a first-year student, started experiencing symptoms of a possible STI. But she was too afraid to visit her local clinic. The nurses knew her family, and she worried her parents would find out. Instead, she searched online, tried home remedies she saw on social media, and waited it out. By the time she got proper treatment, the infection had worsened.

Cultural silence doesn't protect learners and students, and it leaves them vulnerable. Non-judgmental spaces should be available where students feel empowered to ask questions, access care, and make informed choices about their health and bodies.

2. Safe Sex & Protection: What Every Student Should Know

Birth Control & Emergency Contraception

There are various contraceptive options available to help prevent unplanned pregnancies.

These include:

- Birth control pills – taken daily to prevent ovulation.

- Injections – administered every 2-3 months.

- IUDs (Intrauterine Devices) – long-term, low-maintenance protection that can last several years.

- Implants (Implanon) - inserted under the skin of the arm and lasts for 3 to 5 years.

Emergency contraception, often called the *'morning-after pill,'* is designed for unexpected situations, such as when a condom breaks during sexual intercourse or when there is no protection used. It works best when taken within 72 hours after unprotected sex, but the sooner after sex, the better. It is not meant to be a regular birth control method but an important backup.

STIs & Protection

Sexually Transmitted Infections like HIV, chlamydia, gonorrhea, and HPV are more common than many learners and students think and often do not show obvious symptoms at first. Condoms, both male and female, are the most effective way to reduce the risk of STIs during sex. They are not just about pregnancy prevention but about protecting your health.

Regular testing is essential. It is not about shame but about responsibility. Knowing your status means you can take action early, protect your partners, and take control of your health. Protection matters, and testing is not just smart; and it is non-negotiable.

Consent & Sexual Autonomy

Consent is clear, voluntary, and ongoing. If someone is drunk, unconscious, or feels pressured – it is not consent. If it is not a "Hell Yes!" It is a 'No'.

For Nthabiseng, the scariest part was not just what happened to her, and it was not knowing what to do next. Sadly, she wasn't alone.

3. Where to Get Help: Sexual Health Resources for Students

Campus Health Clinics

Offer contraception, STI testing, and confidential consultations.

Marie Stopes South Africa

Helpline: 0800 11 77 85

Provides sexual health services, pregnancy options, and emergency contraception.

Lovelife South Africa

Helpline: 0800 121 900

Focuses on sexual education, STI prevention, and HIV awareness for young people.

Thuthuzela Care Centres (For Sexual Assault Survivors)

Helpline: 0800 428 428

Provides medical care, counseling, and legal assistance for GBV survivors.

For Nthabiseng, knowing this earlier could have changed everything because when it comes to sexual health, ignorance is not harmless, it is dangerous. Knowledge is not just power; and it is protection.

Interactive Element: Knowing Your Sexual Health

Survey Insight:

"I wish I had known more about sexual health before university. I learned things the hard way."

- Have you ever hesitated to ask questions about sexual health out of fear or embarrassment?

- What's one thing you can do today to be more informed and take control of your well-being?

Substance Abuse: The Hidden Epidemic

Nthabiseng never thought she had a drinking problem. She was not the type to wake up craving alcohol. She did not drink alone or hide bottles under her bed. She just drank when everyone else did.

A few drinks to "loosen up" before a night out.

A shot (or five) to match her friends' energy.

A little something to "calm her nerves" before a big exam.

It was normal. Everyone did it. But after that night, the night she woke up with a stranger in an unfamiliar bed with no memory of what happened, she began to wonder:

'When did my choices stop being my own?'

'Was it really just "fun" if I couldn't even remember it?'

'How many other students were falling into the same pattern without even realizing it?'

She had never seen herself as 'someone with a problem,' but after that night, she understood.

It was not just about addiction. It was about blurred lines. It was about losing control without realizing it.

4. The Culture of Drinking & Drug Use on Campus

For many students, substance use isn't seen as a problem.

"Drinking is just part of the university experience..."

"Everyone experiments in college..."

"One night won't hurt..."

But when does 'experimentation' become something more dangerous?

Patterns of Substance Abuse in Colleges and Universities:

- **Binge Drinking** – Consuming large amounts of alcohol in short periods, leading to blackouts and loss of control.

- **Peer Pressure & Social Drinking** – Feeling the need to 'keep up' with friends to fit in.

- **Study Drugs (Ritalin, Adderall, etc.)** – Using prescription stimulants to 'boost' academic performance.

- **Mixing Substances** – Combining alcohol, recreational drugs, and prescription pills increases the risk of overdosing.

Many students do not even realize they have crossed the line into substance abuse until something bad happens, as it did with Nthabiseng.

5. The Dangers Beyond the Buzz

Loss of Control

Alcohol and substance use can lead to blackouts, memory gaps, and impaired decision-making. In that state, your ability to give or withhold consent is compromised, and that is when things can go very wrong. When you are not fully in control of your body or your choices, you become more vulnerable to risky sexual encounters, regret, and even gender-based violence.

It is not just about making 'bad choices' but about not being able to make choices at all. The consequences can last long after the night ends. Understanding your limits, recognizing the signs of intoxication, and having a safety plan with friends are not just precautions, they are protection.

Health Risks

The effects of alcohol and substance use are not always immediate, but they are real. Alcohol poisoning can happen faster than people think, especially when mixing drinks or binge drinking in a short space of time. Addiction often starts subtly – a few drinks to unwind, then needing more to cope. Behind the scenes, mental health struggles like anxiety, depression, and shame can grow, especially after a traumatic and confusing experience.

The danger is not just in the one bad night. It is in what builds slowly, unnoticed, until it gets overwhelming.

Academic Consequences

Substance use and risky behavior do not just affect your nights out but follow you into the classroom. Missed lectures. Late submissions. Failed assignments. For some students, one rough weekend spirals into missed tests or warnings from lecturers. For others, it means losing a bursary or scholarship – not because they were not smart enough, but because their focus slipped.

Academic dreams do not always collapse overnight. Sometimes, they unravel bit-by-bit under the weight of avoidable choices.

Legal Trouble

For many students, one bad decision can have lasting consequences, not just socially but legally.

David had dreams of becoming an engineer. He was focused, ambitious, and on track for a bursary renewal. However, one night, after drinking with friends, he decided to drive back to campus. He was pulled over by the police, arrested, and charged with drunken driving.

The legal process was overwhelming – court dates, fines, and a permanent mark on his record.

His bursary? Gone. The trust of his family? Shaken. His future? Suddenly uncertain. Thousands of students face similar situations every year, not because they are bad people but because no one ever took the time to explain the real-life consequences to them.

Legal trouble does not just threaten your record. It can threaten everything you have worked for.

Increased Risk of Assault & Exploitation

Substances like alcohol, weed, pills, or party drugs do not just cloud your judgment but can blur the ability to give or understand consent. Too many stories start with 'I don't remember' and end in trauma.

Consent is not just about saying 'yes' but also being in a state where you can say it freely, clearly, and consciously. Under the influence, that becomes impossible.

For Nthabiseng, her wake-up call came too late, but for others, there is still time to ask questions, set boundaries, and recognize the risks before they spiral into regret or danger.

Prevention starts before the first sip, puff, or pill.

6. Where to Get Help: Substance Abuse Recovery & Support

SANCA (South African National Council on Alcoholism & Drug Dependence)

Helpline: 011 892 3829

Offers counseling, addiction treatment, and rehab services.

Alcoholics Anonymous South Africa

Helpline: 0861 435 722

Support groups for those struggling with alcohol dependency.

Student Support Services or Wellness Centres

Many campuses offer free counseling for students facing substance abuse challenges.

Peer Support Groups

Talking to someone who understands can make a huge difference.

Nthabiseng wasn't sure if she had a 'problem,' but she knew that her relationship with alcohol had put her in danger, and that was something she could never ignore again.

Interactive Element: Are You in Control?

Survey Insight:

"I never thought I was drinking too much—until I started waking up with regrets."

Reflection Prompt:

- Have you ever felt pressured to drink or use substances just to fit in?

- What's one small change you can make to stay in control of your choices?

As Nthabiseng pieced together the fragments of that night, a chilling realization sank in:

This was not just about alcohol. It was not just about losing control. This was also about what had been done to her while she was vulnerable because alcohol did not just cloud her judgment, it also made her an easier target.

And that is how she ended up here. Lost, confused, and unsure if what had happened to her was even her fault.

She was not alone.

Nthabiseng sat on the edge of her bed, her phone clutched tightly in her hands. She wanted to call someone. Anyone...but what would she even say?

'Would they believe her?'

'Was it really assault if she had been drinking?'

'Was it her fault?'

The shame crept in before the words could form. And the silence felt safer than the judgment she feared. What happened to Nthabiseng was not just a bad night. It was not a mistake. It was not her fault. It was gender-based violence (GBV), a violation of her body, her rights, and her sense of safety. This is a reality faced by countless women, queer individuals, and gender non-conforming students on campuses across the world.

Too often, the weight of GBV is carried in silence – buried under self-blame, societal shame, or disbelief from the very people meant to help. This silence protects no one except the perpetrators. Breaking the cycle begins with truth-telling, naming the violence for what it is. With saying out loud: *"You did not deserve this, you are not alone, and healing is possible."* Until we can speak openly about GBV, we cannot dismantle the culture that enables it.

7. Understanding GBV: It's More Than Physical Abuse

What is Gender-Based Violence (GBV)?

Gender-based Violence is any harm or abuse directed at someone because of their gender, gender identity, or how others perceive their gender. It is not just about physical violence but includes emotional manipulation, sexual assault, verbal threats, financial control, and psychological abuse. Anyone can be affected, but women, girls, Lesbian,

121

Gay, Bisexual, Transgender Queer and plus (LGBTQII+ individuals are most at risk.

Forms of GBV That Happen on Campus:

Sexual Assault & Harassment

This includes rape, unwanted touching, coercion, catcalling, or persistent sexual advances.

Emotional & Psychological Abuse

Using manipulation, threats, or shame to control to belittle someone is often based on harmful gender stereotypes.

Dating & Intimate Partner Violence

Physical harm, emotional blackmail, or controlling behavior within romantic or sexual relationships.

Revenge Porn & Digital Harassment

Sharing private images without consent, stalking through messages or social media, or online bullying.

Corrective Rape & LGBTQI+ Violence

Hate-driven attacks or forced "correction" targeting someone for their sexual orientation or gender identity.

Nthabiseng had never thought of herself as a 'victim,' but now? She was living proof of how easily someone can go from student to statistic.

8. Why So Many Survivors Stay Silent

Even though GBV is common on campuses, most survivors never report it.

Why?

Fear of Being Blamed

"You shouldn't have been drinking."

"You must have led him on."

"Are you sure it wasn't just a misunderstanding?"

Too many survivors hear these words and stay silent.

Shame & Guilt

Many survivors question themselves:

"Did I lead them on?"

"Maybe I overreacted."

"It wasn't that bad."

Lack of Support Systems

Some colleges and universities lack safe, accessible ways for survivors to report abuse, leaving them feeling isolated, unheard, and unprotected.

Fear of Retaliation

Many survivors worry about being threatened, discredited, or shamed if they come forward.

Nthabiseng thought about all these things, and for a long time, she told herself to just move on. Deep inside, though, she knew that staying silent would not make it go away. Pretending it never happened would not erase it, and if she never spoke up, he could do it to someone else.

9. How We Break the Cycle of GBV

Empowering Survivors to Speak Up

Your story matters, your silence does not mean it did not happen, it means you survived!

Speaking up is not easy. It takes strength to name what happened, especially in environments where survivors are blamed, shamed, or ignored. However, every voice that rises breaks a piece of the silence that protects abusers.

Empowerment does not just start with going public but can begin with telling trusted friends, accessing counseling services, or reporting anonymously. The first step is yours to define, and you do not have to take it alone. When survivors feel heard, believed, and supported, healing becomes possible. When enough voices are raised, systems start to shift. Support starts with us. When students look out for one another – by checking in, speaking up, and standing together – campuses become safer for everyone.

Holding Perpetrators Accountable

As a society, we must go beyond awareness campaigns and hashtags. We need to ensure that perpetrators of GBV are thoroughly investigated, held accountable, and face appropriate consequences.

This includes survivor-centered reporting systems, trained disciplinary panels, and zero tolerance for retaliation.

Challenging Rape Culture & Victim-Blaming

What we say – and don't say – shapes the way survivors are treated and how violence is either normalized or condemned.

Instead of: "*What was she wearing?*"

Say: "*Why did he think he had the right to violate her?*"

Instead of: "*Why didn't they fight back?*"

Say: "*Survival looks different for everyone – no one owes you a certain reaction to trauma.*"

Changing rape culture means holding space for survivors without judgment and shifting the blame from those who are harmed to those who cause harm. It means teaching empathy, consent, and respect – not fear, shame and silence.

Creating Safe Spaces for Survivors

Everyone deserves to feel heard, believed, and supported – especially after experiencing trauma.

LGBTQI+ individuals and women need intentional, judgment-free spaces on campus where they can speak without fear of being silenced, blamed, or re-traumatized.

Safe spaces can look like:

- Confidential support groups led by trained counselors or peers.

- Inclusive wellness centers with staff who understand gender-based violence.

- Peer-run initiatives where survivors can share their stories and access resources.

- Online platforms or forums with anonymity for those who aren't ready to speak openly.

Safety isn't just about physical security – it's about emotional and psychological safety, too. When survivors feel seen and supported, healing becomes possible.

Education & Prevention

Education is our first line of defense. When students are equipped with the right knowledge, they're empowered to make safer choices and intervene when it matters most.

Universities and colleges should mandate comprehensive education programs that include:

- Consent education that goes beyond "no means no" and teaches respect, boundaries, and communication.

- Active bystander training so students know how to safely intervene when they witness potential harm.

- GBV awareness programs unpack stereotypes, challenge harmful norms, and promote gender equality.

But education shouldn't be a once-off session during orientation. It must be ongoing, inclusive, and embedded into campus culture – from classrooms to residence halls.

Because prevention doesn't start after harm has happened – it starts with what we teach and how we talk every single day.

Nthabiseng didn't have all the answers.

She didn't know what healing looked like yet.

Silence had protected him, not her.

And she was done with that.

Because the only way to stop the cycle?

It is to break it.

10. Where to Get Help: GBV Resources & Reporting

Thuthuzela Care Centres (For Survivors of Sexual Assault)

Helpline: 0800 428 428

Provides medical, legal, and psychological support for survivors of GBV.

Rape Crisis Cape Town Trust

Helpline: 021 447 9762

Offers counseling, legal advice, and survivor support services.

People Opposing Women Abuse (POWA)

Helpline: 011 642 4345

Provides shelter, therapy, and legal services for women experiencing GBV.

University GBV Taskforces & Campus Police

Many universities have dedicated GBV task forces—students should know how to access them.

For Nthabiseng, these resources would have changed everything.

And for others, knowing where to turn could mean the difference between suffering in silence and reclaiming their power.

Interactive Element: Breaking the Silence

Survey Insight:

"I was afraid to report what happened to me because I thought no one would believe me. No survivor should ever feel that way."

Reflection Prompt:

- What can you do to support survivors and create safer spaces on campus?

- How can we change the conversation around victim-blaming and GBV awareness?

Nthabiseng had spent weeks replaying that night, questioning every choice she had made.

But now, she knew the truth:

She didn't ask for it.

She didn't deserve it.

And she wasn't alone.

The real issue wasn't her outfit, her choices, or the fact that she trusted someone.

The real issue?

A culture that protects perpetrators and blames survivors.

And that's what needs to change.

The Interconnection: How the Toxic Trio Feeds Each Other

Nthabiseng sat in the university wellness office, staring at the poster on the wall.

"Consent. Alcohol. Safety. What You Don't Know Can Hurt You"

She let out a bitter laugh.

If only she had known the signs sooner.

She had walked into that party thinking it would be a night of fun.

She had taken those drinks because it was "just part of the experience."

She had woken up the next morning questioning everything.

And now, as she sat across from the counselor, she was realizing something terrifying.

◆ Her story wasn't unique.

◆ This cycle was happening to students everywhere.

◆ And nobody was talking about it.

The more she thought about it, the more she saw how everything was connected.

Substances lowered her awareness.

Lowered awareness led to risky, unsafe situations.

Those situations made her vulnerable to assault.

The trauma of being assaulted made her want to drink more—to forget.

It's a self-feeding cycle.

One that kept repeating itself until someone found the strength to break free.

1. How Substance Use Increases Risky Sexual Behavior & GBV

Alcohol and drugs don't just affect decision-making.

They alter power dynamics.

Alcohol & Drug Use Lower Inhibitions

What starts as "just one drink" can lead to:

- Unprotected sex – forgetting or choosing not to use condoms or other protection.

- Risky situations - engaging in sexual activity you wouldn't consent to while sober.

- Impaired judgment – missing red flags, struggling to say "no," or misreading someone else's boundaries.

Substance Use & Sexual Assault

Some perpetrators intentionally target individuals who are intoxicated because:

Impaired resistance – they're less able to physically or verbally defend themselves.

Memory gaps - they may not remember details of what happened clearly, making it harder to report.

Internalized blame - they are more likely to question themselves or feel responsible even though it's never their fault.

"Everyone is doing it."

That phrase fuels pressure to say yes – even when you're unsure.

- Casual sex without clear boundaries.

- Substance-fueled hookups where consent is assumed, not asked.

- Blurred lines where "no" isn't respected – or even heard.

Nthabiseng had never thought of herself as someone who took risks.

But now, she realized—sometimes, the risks find you.

2. How GBV Survivors Turn to Substance Use as a Coping Mechanism

When something traumatic happens, sometimes the mind just wants to forget.

To numb the pain.

To feel *something* – or nothing at all.

And for many survivors of gender-based violence, substance use becomes the escape.

Escaping Trauma Through Drugs & Alcohol

Sexual assault. Intimate partner violence. Harassment.

These experiences don't just leave bruises - they leave emotional wounds that are harder to see.

For some students, alcohol or drugs aren't about fun. They're about surviving the sleepless nights.

Quieting the flashbacks.

Numbing the shame.

But the relief is temporary – and the cycle can be devastating.

The Self-Blame Cycle

Survivors often carry questions that haunt them louder than the event itself.

"If I hadn't been drinking, would this have happened?"

"Did I lead them on?"

"Was it my fault?"

Instead of placing blame where it belongs – on the perpetrator – many survivors turn inward, questioning their choices, their memory, and their worth.

And this silence, this shame, feeds the cycle.

The more they blame themselves, the harder it becomes to reach out, to speak up, to heal.

From Casual Use to Dependence

It starts with "just one drink to forget."

Or a pill to sleep.

Or a joint to quiet the noise.

Then another. And another.

Until the pain is replaced by a different kind of numbness – one that doesn't heal just hides.

For Nthabiseng, that moment of realization hit like a slap. Not just because of how far she'd spiraled but because she didn't even notice it happening.

She wasn't just struggling with what had happened to her.

She was struggling with how she was handling it.

The silence. The substance use. The slipping grades.

Everything felt like it was unraveling – and she didn't know how to stop it.

3. Breaking the Cycle

For students stuck in the Toxic Trio, the hardest part isn't realizing something's wrong - it's knowing how to get out.

Educating Yourself & Others

Awareness is the first step.

When students understand how substance use, risky sex, and GBV are interconnected, they're better equipped to protect themselves – and each other.

Knowledge doesn't just break cycles. It builds communities that care, act, and change.

Recognizing Early Warning Signs

If you or someone you know is:

Drinking or using substances to cope or escape

Overlooking red flags in a relationship

Engaging in unprotected sex without thinking about the consequences

It's more than just a phase – it's a signal. A sign that something deeper needs attention.

The sooner you notice the pattern, the sooner you can shift the outcome.

Creating Safer Social Environments

Safety isn't just personal – it's collective.

Look out for your friends and peers.

Step in or seek help when something doesn't feel right.

Speak up - even when it's uncomfortable.

Because changing campus culture starts with everyday choices – and all it takes is one voice to make a difference.

Accessing Support Services

Whether it's therapy, medical care, or peer support – reaching out isn't a sign of weakness. It's a step toward healing. The earlier you ask for help, the easier it is to prevent things from spiraling.

Nthabiseng's eyes flickered over the list of support groups on the counselor's desk. She wasn't sure if she was ready to talk.

But for the first time, she wasn't running from the idea either.

Because she realized that breaking the cycle wasn't just about what had happened to her - It was about what she chose to do next.

Interactive Element: Recognizing the Patterns

Survey Insight:

"I never saw the pattern—until I became part of it. Now, I realize awareness is everything."

Reflection Prompt:

- Have you ever noticed how risky situations rarely happen in isolation? Substance use, unsafe sex, and gender-based violence often overlap. Why do you think that is?

- **What's one real action** you can take today to **break the cycle** in *your* life or campus community?

- Have you ever witnessed a situation that didn't feel right? How did you respond – and how might you respond differently now?

- If someone close to you experienced GBV, would they feel safe telling you? What can you do to make sure they would?

- What myths or messages have you heard about sex, consent, or alcohol that need challenging?

Building a Safety Plan

Nthabiseng had spent weeks feeling powerless.

What had happened to her was out of her control.

The regrets, the shame, the self-doubt—they had all buried her under a weight she couldn't shake.

But then, something changed.

She realized that while she couldn't undo the past, she could take back control of her future.

That's when she decided She needed a safety plan.

Because the truth was, prevention wasn't just about luck—it was about awareness.

And that's when she decided: **She wasn't going to let fear define her future.**

What is a Safety Plan?

A safety plan is a personal strategy designed to reduce harm, avoid high-risk situations, and ensure support is accessible when you need it. It's not about paranoia – it's about preparation.

Steps to Build Your Safety Plan:

1. Safer Socializing: How to Protect Yourself & Friends

Know Your Limits Before Going Out

Decide how much you're comfortable drinking before you even leave the house. If you're at a party, alternate alcohol with water—stay in control.

Never Leave Your Drink Unattended

Spiking drinks is real, and it happens more often than people think.

If you set your drink down and look away, get a new one.

If someone offers you a drink that is already open, decline it.

Use the Buddy System

Always go out with friends you trust, and leave together.

If someone in your group is too drunk to make safe decisions, step in.

Have a Code Word for Unsafe Situations

Agree on a signal or phrase with friends that means: *"Get me out of here."*

Example: "Let's go grab some fresh air" could mean: *"I don't feel safe—help me leave."*

Trust Your Gut—If Something Feels Off, It Probably Is

If someone's behavior makes you uncomfortable, listen to that feeling.

It's always okay to say no—to another drink, to a conversation, to a situation.

Nthabiseng wished she had thought about these things before that night.

She couldn't change what happened to her.

But she could make sure it didn't happen again.

2. Creating a Personal Safety Checklist

Before Going Out:

Set a drinking limit and stick to it.

Charge your phone and ensure you have data and airtime.

Share your location with a trusted friend or family member.

Wear something you feel comfortable and safe in.

During Social Events:

Watch your drink at all times.

Check in with your friends regularly.

Stay aware of your surroundings.

Be mindful of who you engage with—watch for red flags.

If You Feel Unsafe:

Find a trusted friend and remove yourself from the situation.

Call for a ride (Uber, Bolt, or a trusted driver).

Seek out security or event staff if necessary.

If you need immediate help, call an emergency line.

For Nthabiseng, writing this checklist down felt empowering.

It wasn't just about surviving the past.

It was about owning her future.

3. Encouraging Campus-Wide Safety Initiatives

Nthabiseng knew she wasn't the only one who had gone through something like this.

So why was no one talking about it?

She decided to do something bigger than just protecting herself.

She got involved in her university's safety committee, pushing for:

Consent & Safe Sex Education Workshops

Educating students on sexual health, substance use, and GBV prevention.

Stronger Campus Security Measures

Installing better lighting in high-risk areas around campus.

Increasing safe transport options for students after late-night events.

"Safe Nights Out" Campaigns

Encouraging students to use buddy systems and report unsafe behavior.

Partnering with local bars and clubs to promote anti-drink-spiking awareness.

Anonymous Reporting Systems for Assault & Harassment

Making it easier for survivors to report incidents without fear of retaliation.

For the first time since that night, Nthabiseng felt hope.

Because safety wasn't just an individual responsibility.

It was something that every student, friend, and institution needed to take seriously.

And if enough people stood together to demand better protections—change was possible.

Interactive Element: Building Your Own Safety Plan

Survey Insight:

"I never thought about making a safety plan before. But now, I realize it's not about expecting danger—it's about being prepared for anything."

Reflection Prompt:

- What are three personal safety strategies you can start using right now?

- How can you and your friends look out for each other more effectively?

Resources and Support Systems

Nthabiseng sat in her room, staring at the half-empty bottle on her desk.

She had sworn she wouldn't drink tonight.

"Just to take the edge off," she told herself.

But what edge was she trying to soften?

The memories that haunted her every time she closed her eyes?

The weight of a secret she hadn't told anyone?

The feeling that no matter what she did, she would never be the same again?

She turned her phone over, staring at the emergency helpline she'd saved last week.

Thuthuzela Care Centre – GBV Helpline

SANCA – Addiction Support

Campus Wellness Centre – Counseling & Medical Aid

She had looked at those numbers a dozen times - but had never dialed.

Because what if—

They didn't believe her?

They told her she should have been more careful.

Asking for help meant admitting she was broken.

Her hand trembled as it hovered over the call button.

She had spent weeks convincing herself she could handle this alone.

But deep inside, she knew the truth:

She was drowning.

And she needed to reach for a lifeline.

She inhaled sharply, then pressed the call button.

1. The Fear of Asking for Help

The first time Nthabiseng thought about seeing a counselor, she laughed bitterly.

"I'm not crazy."

"Other people have had it worse."

"Talking won't change anything."

But now, as she sat across from a soft-spoken therapist at the university wellness center, she felt the words slip from her lips before she could stop them:

"I don't know who I am anymore."

The counselor didn't flinch.

She just nodded, handing Nthabiseng a cup of warm tea.

"That's okay," she said. "We'll figure it out together."

2. Finding the Right Support: Where to Turn

Campus Health & Wellness Centers

She had walked past the clinic doors a hundred times. But today, she finally stepped inside.

A receptionist greeted her warmly:

"Are you here for a general consultation?"

Nthabiseng hesitated.

"I think... I need to talk to someone."

GBV & Sexual Assault Recovery Services

For weeks, she had whispered the same question to herself: *Was it my fault?*

Until a woman at Thuthuzela Care Centre looked her in the eye and said:

"You did not deserve this. And you are not alone."

Substance Abuse Support Programs

One day, she found herself outside SANCA's office, staring at the door.

She wasn't an "addict," was she? But then she heard someone say:

"You don't have to be at rock bottom to ask for help."

And that's when she walked inside.

For the first time since that night, Nthabiseng felt hope - because asking for help wasn't a weakness.

It was the bravest thing she had ever done.

3. The Power of Community: You Are Not Alone

A week later, Nthabiseng found herself sitting in a small circle of strangers.

It was her first support group meeting.

She felt out of place.

Until the girl next to her—a quiet-looking student with tired eyes—spoke.

"I thought I had to handle everything alone. But the moment I reached out, I realized I had a whole community ready to support me."

Nthabiseng exhaled.

She wasn't the only one.

Survivor-Led Healing Circles

The first time she walked into the support group, she expected judgment.
Instead, she heard stories that sounded just like hers.

Sober Socializing & Safe Campus Nights

She found out about a student-led initiative that helped people get home safely after parties.

"If this had existed before," she thought, "maybe I wouldn't be here now."

Bystander Intervention Training

One of the biggest lessons she learned?

People saw what was happening that night—but no one stepped in.

She vowed to make sure that never happened to someone else.

Because change starts when people decide to care.

And now, she cared more than ever.

Interactive Element: Finding Your Safe Space

Survey Insight:

"I thought I had to handle everything alone. But the moment I reached out, I realized I had a whole community ready to support me."

Reflection Prompt:

- What's one resource or support system you can reach out to today?

- How can you encourage others to seek help when they need it?

Reflections and Takeaways

Nthabiseng sat at the edge of the campus lake, her journal resting on her lap, untouched.

The sun was setting, casting orange and pink reflections on the water. Students walked past her, laughing, talking, and planning their nights. Living.

She exhaled.

For weeks, she had felt like an outsider looking in.

Like a ghost walking among people who didn't know she was breaking inside.

She traced her fingers over the worn edges of the journal her counselor had given her.

"Write down what you've learned from this experience."

She scoffed. *Learned?*

What had she learned, really?

That life could turn upside down in one night?

Sometimes, your biggest regrets aren't the choices you made but the ones you never got to make.

That even when you scream inside, the world keeps moving like nothing happened.

Her fingers tightened around the pen.

She wanted to erase that fateful night. To undo it. To forget all about it.

But maybe... forgetting wasn't the goal anymore.

Maybe healing was.

1. The Hardest Lessons She Learned

Lesson 1: You Can't Heal What You Refuse to Face.

She had spent weeks outrunning the memories. Drowning herself in distractions, in alcohol, in silence.

But pain doesn't disappear. It waits.

Lesson 2: Your Worth Isn't Defined by What Happened to You.

For a long time, she had wondered if that night had rewritten her entire   identity.
If she would always just be "the girl who lost control."

But no. She was still Nthabiseng. Still smart, still strong, still her.

Lesson 3: You Are Not Alone—Even When It Feels Like You Are.

The first time she sat in that support group circle, she felt like a fraud.

"I shouldn't be here. Other people have been through worse."

But then she heard someone say:

"Some nights, I lie awake thinking about everything. And I wonder... will I ever feel normal again?"

At that moment, Nthabiseng realized she wasn't the only one.

2. The Choice to Heal

She stared at the blank page in her journal.

"Write what you've learned."

She hesitated, then pressed her pen to the paper.

"Healing isn't about pretending it never happened."

"It's learning to live with what happened."

"And I am still here."

She stopped, her breath catching in her throat.

I am still here.

Three simple words. But they hit her harder than anything else she had written.

She closed the journal gently, carefully—like something sacred.

Because for the first time since that night, she didn't just write those words.

She believed them.

3. Moving Forward: What Every Student Needs to Remember

Nthabiseng stood up, hugging the journal to her chest.

She turned back toward campus; toward the life she had put on pause for too long.

Lesson 1: Awareness is Power.

She had learned that **se**xual health, substance use, and GBV weren't just random dangers—they were interconnected.

Lesson 2: Looking Out for Others Can Change Lives.

The difference between a safe night out and a dangerous one is often one friend stepping in.

Lesson 3: Healing Isn't Linear, But It Is Possible.

Whether it is therapy, journaling, support groups, or just taking it day by day—it all counts.

She reached into her bag, pulling out her phone.

Thuthuzela Care Centre – GBV Helpline

SANCA – Addiction Support

Campus Wellness Centre – Counseling & Medical Aid

She had saved these numbers weeks ago.

Tonight, she was sending them to someone else.

Because if she could help even one person find the courage to ask for help, everything she went through would mean something.

She pressed send.

Interactive Element: Your Own Reflections

Survey Insight:

"The biggest lesson I learned is that I don't have to heal alone. And neither do you."

- What's one thing you've discovered about yourself during tough times?

- How might that insight help you move forward with more strength?

Your Story Is Still Being Written

As Nthabiseng stood up from the park bench, she took one last deep breath.

For so long, she had been waiting—waiting for the pain to go away, waiting to feel like herself again, waiting to turn back time.

But now, she understood something she hadn't before.

- Healing isn't rewriting the past.

- It's reclaiming the future.

- You are not what happened to you.

She had survived the worst days of her life. And now she was ready to start living again.

Her story isn't over.

And neither is yours.

Chapter 7:

Beyond Compliance: Creating a Culture of Inclusion For Learners with Disabilities

Breaking Barriers

Sindi stood at the entrance of the lecture hall, gripping her cane so tightly her knuckles turned white.

The air inside was thick with anticipation, the rustling of papers, the scraping of chairs, and the familiar buzz of students chatting before class.

"You've done this before. Just breathe."

But today wasn't like before.

Today, she walked in alone.

She exhaled, tilting her head slightly as she focused on the sounds around her. Every noise painted a picture.

A group of students laughed near the back row—probably the same ones who always whispered during class. The squeak of the professor's shoes as he paced near the podium, shuffling through notes.

A chair dragging against the floor—a seat was open.

"Four steps forward, then turn left."

Her fingers tightened around her cane as she moved forward carefully, navigating a world built for sighted people.

1. Navigating a Campus Built for Others

Every day, Sindi faced invisible barriers that no one else noticed.

Lecture halls weren't designed for students like her. Campus libraries had shelves of books—but few in braille or digital format. Professors used slides and diagrams without explaining them aloud.

For others, it was as simple as looking at the board.

For Sindi, it meant hours of extra effort just to keep up.

She could still hear the voice of one lecturer from her first semester:

"Sorry, Sindi, I don't have an accessible version of the textbook. Can you try to manage?"

She smiled politely and nodded.

"I'll manage," she had said.

But inside?

She had wanted to scream.

"Why should I have to work twice as hard for the same education?"

Yet, she never let herself dwell on it. She didn't have time to be angry.

She had to keep moving, keep adjusting, and keep proving that she belonged here.

Because if she didn't fight for herself, who would?

2. Moments of Triumph: When Determination Wins

One evening, after a particularly frustrating day, Sindi collapsed onto her bed, exhausted.

She had spent hours struggling to access her assignment.

The university's online learning portal wasn't compatible with her screen reader.

The professor's response had been frustratingly dismissive: *"Just do your best."*

Her best?

Her best was staying up late every night, grappling with how to find alternative ways to study.

Her best was fighting for access to materials others took for granted.

Her best was pushing through exhaustion, loneliness, and frustration—just to be on the same level as everyone else.

Tears burned at the back of her eyes, but she blinked them away.

"You can't afford to break."

A sharp knock at the door made her sit up.

"Hey, Sindi? It's Karabo."

She recognized the voice instantly—Karabo, her classmate, someone who had never treated her differently.

"I recorded today's lecture for you," Karabo said, holding out a flash drive. "And I found some accessible study materials. Thought it might help."

Sindi froze.

Her hands trembled as she reached for the flash drive.

"You did this... for me?"

Karabo tilted her head. "Why wouldn't I? You deserve to have the same resources as the rest of us."

For the first time in a long while, the fight didn't feel so lonely.

She wasn't just managing.

She was seen.

She had an ally.

Her fingers curled around the flash drive.

"Thank you."

For the first time that semester, she felt a little less alone.

Understanding the Landscape

Sindi sat in the student lounge, sipping her tea, as a lively discussion unfolded around her.

"I don't think we even have students with disabilities on campus," one student said.

"Yeah, I mean, I've never seen anyone using a wheelchair in our lecture halls," another chimed in.

She almost laughed.

She had heard it before—the assumption that if something isn't visible, it doesn't exist.

She let her fingers rest lightly on her white cane, tracing its familiar grip.

"We're here," she finally said, her voice steady. "You just don't see us."

The room fell silent.

Some shifted awkwardly in their seats. Others glanced at her, curious.

"You don't see us—not because we're not here, but because this campus was never built with us in mind."

She could feel their discomfort—the realization that accessibility wasn't just ramps and elevators.

It was representation. Awareness. A seat at the table.

And most importantly?

It was about breaking the silence.

1. The Reality of Disability Representation in Higher Education

The numbers don't lie—but they reveal a painful truth.

- **Less than 2%**—that's how many students with disabilities make it to universities and TVET colleges in South Africa. And the ones who do? They don't just study. They fight. Every single day.

- In many institutions, only a fraction of campus buildings is fully accessible.

- There are little to no assistive technologies in classrooms, leaving students to find solutions on their own.

Why don't we see more students with disabilities?

- Many never make it to higher education due to a lack of accessible schooling.

- Campus environments create invisible barriers that push students out.

- Some students hide their disabilities for fear of discrimination.

Sindi had learned these truths firsthand.

She had lost count of how many times she had to fight for what was freely given to others.

"Why don't you just record the lectures and listen later?"

"We don't have braille textbooks, but can't you just have someone read to you?"

"Are you sure you can handle a university workload?"

Each question felt like another wall placed in front of her.

And she was tired of having to break them down alone.

2. More Than Just Physical Barriers: The Weight of Stigma

Being visually impaired isn't just about navigating spaces.

It's also about navigating other people's perceptions.

The professors doubted her ability to keep up.

The students pitied her instead of treating her like an equal.

The assumption was that her presence on campus was somehow "inspirational" just for existing.

"People think inclusion is about ramps and elevators," Sindi said, shaking her head.

"But what about dignity? What about respect? They design buildings for us," she continued. "But they don't expect us to walk through the door."

Karabo let out a breath. "So, what does real inclusivity look like?"

Sindi paused, then said, "It looks like not having to fight for every little thing just to get what everyone else already has."

True inclusivity means:

Not being an afterthought.

Not having to explain why you deserve to be here.

Not needing to prove your worth over and over again.

But the hardest truth?

Most people don't think about inclusivity at all—until they are the ones who need it.

Interactive Element: Reflection on Inclusivity

Survey Insight:

"Inclusivity isn't just about making space—it's about making sure everyone feels like they belong in that space."

Reflection Prompt:

- What does inclusivity mean to you?
- How can you make your community more accessible and welcoming?

Accessibility Challenges

Sindi's fingers hovered over the keyboard, her screen reader repeating the words like a cruel echo.

"Error: File not accessible."

Her stomach sank. She refreshed the page.

Still Nothing.

Her professor had uploaded yet another scanned document—another reminder that the system wasn't built for her.

"Again?" she muttered, frustration bubbling inside her.

She clenched her fists, willing herself not to cry, not to scream, not to throw her laptop across the room.

She had fought this battle too many times.

1. When the World Isn't Built for You

Sindi had never asked for special treatment.

She didn't need anyone to pity her.

She didn't want to be an inspiration just for existing.

She just wanted the same access as everyone else.

But every day, she ran into invisible walls—barriers that others never even noticed.

The library had thousands of books, but barely any in braille or digital formats.

Her Residence had steps at the entrance—no tactile paving, no sound cues.

Lecture halls had screens filled with visuals she couldn't see, with no verbal descriptions.

For most students, getting to class was as simple as opening a door.

But for Sindi?

It was an obstacle course—one where the rules weren't made with her in mind.

Every step, every class, every request felt like a fight for basic access.

2. The Policy vs. Reality Gap

Her university had a disability policy.

She had read it.

"We are committed to accessibility and inclusion for all students."

But when she had gone to request lecture notes in an accessible format, the admin officer had looked at her like she was asking for the moon.

154

"We don't really have that system in place yet."

"Can't you just ask a classmate to help?"

"We'll try, but it might take a few weeks."

Weeks?

"Do sight students have to wait weeks for their notes?" she had wanted to ask.

But she didn't.

Because she was tired.

Tired of being the only one asking for change.

3. When Technology Becomes a Lifeline

Not everything was a dead end.

Technology was changing the game—for those who had access. She had discovered screen readers, braille displays, and AI-powered transcription services.

Be My Eyes—an app that connects visually impaired users with volunteers for real-time assistance. **JAWS (Job Access With Speech)**—a software that reads digital text aloud.

Text-to-Speech Scanners—which could convert printed materials into audio.

But these tools weren't cheap. Many students couldn't afford them.

And most universities weren't willing to invest in them.

"If I don't fight for this, who will?" Sindi thought to herself.

"No one is going to fight for you unless you fight first."

And so she did.

She started filing formal complaints.

She pushed for accessible course materials.

She petitioned for better resources on campus.

Because she refused to believe that "just managing" was enough.

She wanted to thrive. She deserved to thrive.

Interactive Element: Spot the Barriers

Survey Insight:

"*Most universities claim to be accessible, but how many actually are?*"

Reflection Prompt:

- Think about your campus. Are there barriers that you've never noticed before?

- What's one change that could make your environment more accessible for everyone?

Creating Inclusive Communities

Sindi walked across the campus courtyard, feeling the heat of the sun on her skin. She could hear the energy around her—students laughing, the hum of conversation, the faint shuffle of footsteps as people moved between classes.

But as she traced her fingers along the edges of her cane, she couldn't shake the heaviness in her chest.

She had fought so many battles alone.

Professors who "forgot" to send accessible notes—again.

A library full of books, yet none in braille.

She sighed of impatience when she asked for accommodations like she was a burden.

She wasn't asking for special treatment. She was asking for a chance to succeed like everyone else. And the truth was, no amount of individual resilience could change a system that wasn't built for her.

"So what would?"

She stopped walking, gripping her cane tightly.

"Community."

She had spent so much time thinking she had to fight alone, but the reality was that real change only happened when people stood together.

And if the system wasn't going to change itself?

Then maybe—it was time to make it change.

1. Awareness: The First Step toward Inclusion

The first time she attended a disability awareness event, she was skeptical.

Would it be another surface-level talk about "supporting people with disabilities" without real action?

Would it be *just for show*—an event where people applauded but never actually changed anything?

But then, she saw the panelists.

A deaf student advocating for sign language interpreters in classrooms.

A wheelchair user speaking about the lack of ramps in key buildings.

A neurodivergent student explaining why timed exams weren't fair for everyone.

And as they shared their struggles, she saw something even more powerful—students without disabilities listening.

Really listening. Taking notes. Asking questions. Wanting to help.

She realized then that change starts with awareness.

When people see the barriers, they start to care. When they care, they take action.

That was the first step.

But awareness without action? That hasn't changed. That was just a conversation.

2. Collaboration: Universities, NGOs & Student Movements

After the event, she met one of the speakers, a student activist named Zayd.

"We're launching an accessibility campaign on campus," he said. "Want to join us?"

Sindi hesitated.

She had spent so long fighting alone.

Could she really trust that others wanted to fight alongside her?

But then she remembered Karabo—the friend who had helped her with lecture notes without being asked. She also recalled the students at the panel discussion—listening, learning, wanting to do better.

Maybe this time, she wouldn't be alone.

She nodded. *"I'm in."*

That semester, they started working with NGOs and advocacy groups.

They pushed the university to fund assistive technology.

They demanded policies that ensured lecture halls were accessible to everyone.

They collaborated with disability rights organizations to improve campus facilities.

Gradually, things started to change.

Change didn't happen because one person fought harder.

It happened because people refused to fight alone.

Because they saw injustice—and chose to stand against it.

3. What True Inclusion Looks Like

One afternoon, Sindi walked into a lecture hall and paused.

Something was different.

She tapped her cane lightly against the floor, moving forward, and then smiled.

Tactile paving. Audio-assisted lecture slides. A new row of accessible seating near the front.

"Looks like we're getting somewhere," Zayd nudged her playfully.

She turned toward him, feeling a warmth in her chest she hadn't felt in a long time.

She had fought for this.

She had believed this was possible—even when no one else did.

And now? It was real.

"Inclusion isn't about words. It's about action," she whispered.

And for the first time since she had started this journey, she truly felt like she belonged.

Interactive Element: How Inclusive Is Your Community?

Survey Insight:

"Inclusivity isn't just about allowing people in—it's about making sure they feel like they belong."

Reflection Prompt:

- What's one step you can take to make your campus or workplace more inclusive?

- Have you ever noticed barriers that others might not see? How can you help break them down?

The Role of Allies and Advocates

Sindi never imagined that a simple conversation in the canteen would change the course of her life. She sat alone, tracing the rim of her coffee cup, drained from another day of proving she belonged.

She thought of the lecture notes she couldn't read. The sideways glances from professors who didn't know how to teach a visually impaired student. The feeling that, no matter how hard she tried, she would always have to work twice as hard just to be on the same playing field.

And then, Zayd sat down across from her.

"You look like you're carrying the world on your back."

She smirked bitterly. "I do. And it's made of stairs, small font, and PDF files I can't read."

Zayd laughed but then grew serious. "That's not fair. What if we did something about it?"

"We?" she asked.

And that was the first time she realized something important—change didn't have to be a solo fight.

1. What Does It Mean to Be an Ally?

Being an ally isn't about sympathy—it's about action. An ally is someone who:

Actively fights alongside them.

Uses their privilege to push for real change.

Doesn't just say, "I support you," but asks, "How can I help?"

Zayd wasn't visually impaired. He didn't know what it was like to walk into a lecture hall and feel completely unconsidered in its design. But he knew something was wrong. More importantly, he knew that his voice, as a sighted student, could amplify Sindi's struggles in places where she wasn't being heard.

That's what allies do.

2. Stories of Successful Allyship

Advocating for Accessible Policies

After that conversation, Sindi and Zayd started something bigger than themselves.

They petitioned the university to fund assistive technologies.

They worked with the student government to ensure lecture slides were accessible to all.

They called out professors who weren't making their courses inclusive.

Standing Against Discrimination

One day, during a heated class discussion, a student muttered under his breath:

"Why do we have to keep adjusting everything for a few people?"

Before Sindi could even react, Zayd spoke up.

"Because inclusion isn't about numbers. It's about making sure every student—every single one—has the same right to learn."

The room fell silent.

That's what allyship looks like.

Speaking up when those affected are too tired to.

3. How You Can Be an Ally

Step 1: Listen. Really Listen.

Don't assume you know what persons living with disability (PLWD) need. True allyship starts with humility and a willingness to learn.

Instead of offering solutions off the bat, ask:

"What are the biggest challenges you face, and how can I support you?"

"How can I support you in a way that supports your choices and needs?

Listen without interrupting. Validate their experiences. Sometimes, just being heard is the most powerful form of support.

Step 2: Use Your Voice.

Call out discrimination when you see it. Speak up in moments that matter – even when it's uncomfortable.

Push for policy changes in your school, workplace, or community.

Your voice can help shift systems that were never built with inclusion in mind.

Step 3: Educate Others.

When someone says something ignorant, don't let it slide - correct them.

Share stories, resources, and initiatives that promote accessibility and inclusion.

Speak up. Show up. And make space for voices that aren't always heard.

Step 4: Support Without Taking Over.

Allies amplify voices – they don't speak over them.

Help their voice carry – don't replace it with your own.

Interactive Element: How Can You Be an Ally?

Survey Insight:

"Allyship isn't about being the hero. It's about standing beside someone and saying, 'I won't let you fight this alone.'"

Reflection Prompt:

- Think about a time you witnessed exclusion or inaccessibility—what could have been done differently?

- What is one action you can take today to support inclusion?

Resources and Support Systems

The first time Sindi searched for disability support services on her university's website, she found nothing useful.

The second time, she emailed the student affairs office.

"We'll get back to you soon," was the response.

Weeks passed.

Silence.

It took three more emails, a trip to the administration office, and an exhausting back-and-forth just to get a meeting with the so-called "student support officer."

She had walked into that office hopeful but walked out realizing that "support" often existed in name only.

1. Campus Disability Services: When Policy Doesn't Match Reality

"We have a disability office," the admin officer said.

"Okay, but where?" Sindi asked.

"Oh, it's under student affairs... somewhere. I think."

That's when she understood the problem.

Universities love to talk about inclusivity. They loved to put it in brochures, policies, and mission statements. But when it came to real implementation?

PLWD were often left behind.

Some colleges and universities have counseling services, but no mental health professionals trained in disability-related trauma. Some campuses provided accommodations, but only after months of paperwork and fighting through red tape. Some classrooms have accessible seating but no adjustments in teaching methods or materials.

She had learned that, in higher education, having a right to accessibility didn't guarantee access.

And that needed to change.

2. Government Grants and NGO-Led Mentorship Programs

Sindi first learned about government funding for students with disabilities from another visually impaired student in a support group.

"Did you apply for the disability bursary?"

She had blinked.

"There's a bursary?"

"Yeah. They don't advertise it well, but it exists. You should check it out."

That night, she spent hours researching.

NSFAS Disability Bursary – Covers assistive technology, tuition, and accommodation.

NSFAS provides funding for students with disabilities, covering essential expenses such as:

Tuition Fees, Accommodation, Meals, Transport, Assistive Devices, and Human Support Services

To qualify, applicants must:

- Be South African citizens

- Registered at a public university or TVET college

- Have a disability requiring additional financial assistance

- Come from a household with a combined income of R600,000 per year or less

- Demonstrate academic potential to pass their coursework

Eligible Disabilities

NSFAS recognizes various disabilities, including:

Neurodevelopmental Disabilities*: Autism and ADHD are recognized under NSFAS, and students may qualify for full tuition, living, and travel allowances

How to Apply

Gather required documents: medical or psychological report, proof of income, ID, and registration documents

Create a MyNSFAS account and apply online

Upload supporting documents and submit application

SASL Access Grants – Supports deaf students needing interpreters.

Private scholarships for students with disabilities – often unpublicized, yet life-changing.

"Why did no one tell me this before?"

The resources existed—hidden in fine print, buried in red tape.

She decided to make it her mission to spread awareness.

Because access isn't a privilege – it's a right. And no student should have to fight for what they already deserve.

3. Online Platforms Offering Guidance and Advocacy

One night, frustrated after another accessibility issue, she stumbled across a Facebook group for students with disabilities.

"Any other blind students struggling with getting accessible materials?" she typed.

Within minutes, her post blew up.

Dozens of students shared similar struggles. Some offered solutions—apps, advocacy strategies, and creative ways to make things work. Others vented their frustration, finally feeling heard.

"Wow. So it's not just me?"

That's when she realized the power of online communities.

Top Online Resources for PLWD:

"Be My Eyes" – Pairs visually impaired users with volunteers for real-time assistance.

"Able2Work" – Offers career mentorship and job opportunities for disabled students.

"Disabled Students South Africa" – An advocacy group pushing for national policy changes in education.

She wasn't alone.

And with the right resources, no one else had to feel alone either.

Interactive Element: Finding Your Support Network

Survey Insight:

"Accessibility is a right, not a privilege. But you'll never get it unless you demand it."

Reflection Prompt:

- What's one resource you've found helpful in overcoming challenges?

- How can you help spread awareness so others don't have to struggle alone?

Stories of Triumph

Sindi stood in the auditorium, gripping the edges of the podium.

The room was packed—students, members of staff, even journalists—all gathered for the annual Student Excellence Awards.

"And the award for Outstanding Student Leadership goes to..."

She had rehearsed this moment so many times in her head.

But as they called her name, she still felt the air leave her lungs.

"Me?"

The applause was deafening. She felt Karabo squeeze her shoulder in encouragement.

"Go. You earned this."

And as she stepped onto the stage, gripping her white cane, she realized something deep in her bones.

This wasn't just her moment.

It was for every student who had been dismissed, overlooked, or made to fight twice as hard just to be seen.

1. The Power of Resilience: Breaking the Expectations

People didn't expect her to succeed.

They had assumed she'd struggle. They had expected her to quit. They had never considered that she could lead.

But she had.

She had gone from being the student who was ignored to being the voice for thousands like her.

"This is for every person who's ever felt unseen. We are here. We always have been."

The crowd exploded in applause again.

She smiled.

Not for herself—but for every student watching who needed to believe that they, too, could rise.

2. Others Who Defied the Odds

Tumelo, the Deaf Engineering Graduate

Tumelo had spent his first year struggling to keep up.

Professors spoke too fast. The captions were unreliable. Interpreters weren't always provided.

"I wanted to quit every single day."

But then, he fought back.

He demanded real-time captions for all online lectures. He worked with professors to ensure clear communication. And graduated top of his class.

Now?

He was leading an initiative to create AI-powered sign language translations for classrooms.

"They told me I couldn't be here. Now I'm making sure the next student won't have to fight as hard as I did."

Lethabo, the Wheelchair Athlete Who Changed University Sports

I've always been a fighter.

I played basketball in high school, until an accident left me paralyzed from the waist down.

"I thought that was it, the end of everything I had worked for. No one told me I could keep playing. So I decided to rewrite the rules."

But I didn't stop.

I petitioned the university to start its first wheelchair basketball team. I pushed for accessible gym facilities. I led the team to win our first national championship.

And now?

I'm on my way to the Paralympics.

"Disability doesn't mean inability. The only thing we lack is opportunity."

3. The Role of Community in Every Triumph

None of these victories happened alone.

Sindi had Karabo, Zayd, and other student advocates.

Tumelo had professors who listened and changed.

Lethabo had a team that believed in her vision.

Every success story had one thing in common: Community.

Because inclusion isn't just about allowing people in.

It's about making sure they have the tools to thrive.

And every time someone stood up and demanded change, they made it easier for the next person.

Interactive Element: Celebrating Your Own Triumphs

Survey Insight:

"Success isn't about overcoming disability—it's about overcoming the barriers that society places in your way."

Gratitude Journal Prompt:

- What is one challenge you've faced and overcome?

- Who was there to support you along the way?

Reflections and Takeaways

Sindi sat under the shade of an old oak tree, her fingers lightly brushing over the cover of her notebook.

The campus buzzed around her—students rushing to class, laughter from a nearby group of friends, and the distant hum of an announcement over the intercom.

She had sat in this exact spot many times before.

On days when she felt like a ghost, present but unseen. When she felt exhausted from fighting battles, no one else saw. And on those days when she wondered if she truly belonged here.

But today felt different.

Because today, for the first time in a long time, she wasn't just surviving.

She was thriving.

1. The Hardest Truths She Had to Learn

Inclusion isn't given. It's fought for.

No one had ever handed her accessibility on a silver platter. She had to demand it, push for it, and advocate for it. And in doing so, she had helped make it easier for students like her.

You don't have to do it alone.

She had spent so long thinking she had to carry it all on her own. But the truth is change happens faster when people stand together.

Her disability was not a weakness.

People had underestimated her. They had questioned her ability to succeed. But in the end, she had proved them wrong—not for them, but for herself.

She traced her fingers over the page and wrote:

"I am more than my struggles. I am my victories."

She smiled.

Because now, she believed it.

2. What This Journey Taught Her About Others

Most people don't think about accessibility until they need it.

She had seen how easy it was for people to ignore issues that didn't affect them.

But she had also seen how powerful it was when people chose to care.

Being an ally means taking action, not just feeling sympathy.

Karabo had shown her that allyship wasn't about "helping." It was about standing beside someone, fighting with them, not for them.

People are willing to learn—if you give them the chance.

She had expected resistance. But more often than not, people just needed someone to open their eyes to the problem.

She had learned that real change doesn't start with policies—it starts with conversations.

3. Moving Forward: What Inclusivity Truly Means

Inclusivity is not just about access. It's about belonging.

It's not enough to allow people in. They need to feel like they are meant to be there, and they need to feel seen, heard, and valued.

It takes all of us to create an inclusive world.

If a classmate had a disability, would you:

- Ignore the barriers they face.
- Or ask how you can support them.

If a university or college policy excluded someone, would you walk past?

- Say, "That's not my problem"?
- Or speak up, even if the issue doesn't affect you directly?

Inclusivity is a choice.

And every person has the power to make that choice.

She flipped to the last page of her notebook and wrote:

"The world won't change on its own. But I can be part of the change."

She closed the book, but not the chapter, because this wasn't the end of her fight.

It was just the start.

Interactive Element: Your Own Reflections

Survey Insight:

"The most powerful thing I learned is that I have the ability to create change—no matter how small."

Journal Prompt:

- What does true inclusivity look like to you?

- How can you actively advocate for a more inclusive world?

Celebrating Abilities

Sindi stood at the front of the auditorium, her cane resting lightly against her leg.

The room was silent, expectant.

A year ago, she wouldn't have imagined standing here—not as a student requesting accommodations, but as a speaker, a leader, a voice for change.

She inhaled deeply, then spoke.

"For so long, conversations about disability have focused on what we lack. On what we cannot do."

"But today, I want to talk about what we can do."

1. Emphasizing Abilities Over Limitations

The world often sees PLWD through a single lens—struggle, dependence, and limitation.

"How do you manage?"

"It *must be so hard.*"

"*I could never do what you do.*"

But Sindi had learned that disability doesn't mean inability.

Tumelo revolutionized assistive learning technology for deaf students.

Lethabo had led her wheelchair basketball team to a national championship.

And she—she had helped change university policies for students like her.

None of them had succeeded because of pity.

They had succeeded because they were given the tools and opportunities to thrive.

And that's what real inclusion looks like.

2. Building a World Where Everyone Belongs

Sindi scanned the crowd, letting her words settle.

"Inclusivity isn't just about access—it's about belonging."

It's about a world where:

- Students don't have to fight for basic accommodations.
- Employers don't hesitate to hire someone based on their disability.
- Society sees beyond the cane, the wheelchair, the hearing aid—to the person.

"We all have a role to play in creating that world."

It isn't about grand gestures. It was about small choices every single day.

Hiring without bias.

Designing spaces that welcome everyone.

Speaking up when accessibility is ignored.

Because inclusion isn't a favor.

It is a right.

3. An Empowering Message of Hope

Sindi paused, then smiled.

"If there's one thing I want you to take from today, it's this:"

We are not defined by what we lack. We are defined by what we bring to the world. And every single one of us—PLWD or not—has something powerful to offer.

The applause started to slow down. Then, it swelled—loud, thunderous, a standing ovation.

She felt warmth spread through her chest.

This was the moment she had once thought impossible.

This was the moment she knew—she belonged.

Interactive Element: How Will You Be Part of the Change?

Survey Insight:

"Inclusion isn't about making space for PLWD—it's about realizing they should have always been part of the space."

Reflection Prompt:

- What is one action you can take to make the world more inclusive?

- How can you challenge your own biases about ability and disability?

Celebrating Abilities

Sindi stood at the center of the stage, her fingers tracing the smooth edges of her cane.

The lights above were bright, warming her skin, but the real heat came from the energy in the room.

Hundreds of students were standing, clapping, cheering.

Professors who once doubted her abilities were now applauding her success. Administrators who had overlooked accessibility issues were now hearing her voice—loud and clear.

She closed her eyes for a second just to take it all in.

A year ago, she had fought just to be heard. Now, the entire room hung on her every word.

She stepped closer to the microphone, her heart pounding.

This was the moment she had dreamed about.

She took a deep breath and spoke.

"For so long, people have looked at disability as a limitation. As a weakness. But I stand before you today—not in spite of my disability, but because of it."

The room fell silent.

"My blindness doesn't make me less capable. It doesn't make me less intelligent. It makes me different. And difference isn't a barrier to success—it's the reason I stand before you today."

1. The Shift from Pity to Power

For too long, the world had pitied people like her.

"How do you manage?"

"It must be so hard."

"You're so inspiring for trying."

She didn't want pity.

She wanted opportunity. She wanted action. She wanted a world that didn't just "accommodate" people like her—but valued them.

Because the truth was—she didn't need the world's sympathy.

She needed its recognition.

2. A Future Where Everyone Belongs

She shifted slightly on stage, gripping the microphone with confidence now.

"Real inclusivity isn't about opening doors—it's about never closing them in the first place."

She could feel the weight of every moment that had led her here:

The nights spent questioning if she was enough.

The exhaustion of fighting for what should have never been denied her and those like her.

The people who stood beside her lifted her up when she was too tired to keep going.

She knew the battle wasn't over.

There were still classrooms without accessibility features. Students were afraid to ask for accommodations.

And barriers standing in the way of people like her.

But change is coming. And that change starts with us.

"It starts when we stop looking at disability as something to "fix" and start seeing it for what it really is—just another way of existing."

3. The Final Message: Ability Is Everywhere

The audience was completely silent now, hanging onto her words.

She inhaled deeply and gave them one final message.

"We are not defined by what we lack. We are defined by what we bring to the world. And ability? It's everywhere—if you're willing to see it."

As she stepped back from the microphone, the room erupted in applause.

But this time, she wasn't just hearing it—she was feeling it.

And as she left the stage, she knew—this wasn't the end of her journey.

It was only the beginning.

Interactive Element: How Will You Be Part of the Change?

Survey Insight:

"Inclusion isn't about making space for PLWD—it's about realizing they should have always been part of the space."

Reflection Prompt:

- What is one action you can take to make the world more inclusive?
- How can you challenge your own biases about ability and disability?

A Final Reflection

As Sindi walked off the stage, she gripped her cane tightly, feeling the warmth of the moment settle inside her.

For years, she had fought to be heard. To be seen. To be included.

And now? She wasn't just part of the conversation—she was leading it.

She turned back for one last glance at the audience, knowing that among them were students just like her, waiting for their moment to step forward.

"This isn't just my victory. It's ours."

"Inclusion isn't just about making space—it's about making sure everyone feels they belong."

And as she stepped down, she knew this wasn't the end of the fight.

It was just the beginning.

Chapter 8:

Navigating Financial Waters

The Budget Blues

Lethabo sat alone at the campus canteen, stirring her coffee absentmindedly. The warmth of the drink did little to ease the cold reality troubling her. Surrounded by her classmates chatting about weekend plans and outings, she felt like an outsider in the world of carefree university life. Her thoughts weren't on the upcoming lecture; instead, they were consumed by the mounting pressure of how she was going to make it through another month.

Coming from a poor background, Lethabo had always known struggle. But this was different. Being at university was a dream come true, but the financial burden was overwhelming. She had carefully planned her budget, trying to account for every expense. But life had other plans. Social pressures crept in—the spontaneous lunch dates, the weekend getaways with friends, the need to fit in. It was easy to get caught up in the moment, to justify spending a little more here and there, but before she knew it, her bank account was dwindling, and her credit card balance was creeping up.

The emotional toll of financial mismanagement was heavy. Lethabo felt the weight of every missed payment and every delayed bill. The stress was taking a toll on her academic focus, as the worry about finances clouded her mind during lectures. The worst part? She wasn't alone. Many students, especially those depending on financial aid, were facing similar struggles.

As she sat there, scrolling through her bank app, Lethabo knew that she needed more than just a budget. She needed financial literacy—the ability to manage her money wisely, plan for the future, and make smarter decisions. And she wasn't the only one. For many students, financial literacy was the key to surviving—and thriving—during their time at college or university.

Understanding Financial Literacy

Financial literacy is more than just balancing a budget—it's about understanding the broader picture of money management. It's about making informed choices that will help you manage your income, control your spending, save for the future, and even invest wisely. For students like Lethabo, financial literacy isn't just a luxury; it's a necessity.

At its core, financial literacy involves the basics of budgeting, saving, and spending wisely. But it goes beyond that. It's about making decisions based on your circumstances, setting goals, and avoiding pitfalls. One of the biggest challenges students face is managing impulsive spending. Whether it's the peer pressure to go out for coffee with friends or the temptation to buy the latest gadget, these little purchases add up and can derail even the most carefully planned budget.

Common Pitfalls of Financial Management:

- **Impulsive Spending** - Buying things you don't need because they're "on sale" or because your friends are doing it.

- **Peer Pressure** - Feeling the need to spend on social outings or experiences just to "fit in."

- **Unnecessary Subscriptions** - The ongoing charges for streaming services or apps that you don't even use.

Recognizing these pitfalls is the first step to avoiding them.

Interactive Exercise: Take a moment to think about your own financial goals. What would you like to achieve this semester? Perhaps it's saving a specific amount, sticking to a budget, or avoiding impulse purchases.

Write them down and keep them in mind as you continue through this chapter. Setting clear goals will help you stay focused and accountable.

Budgeting 101

Creating a budget isn't just about tracking every cent you spend. It's about taking control of your money and making intentional decisions. As a student, especially one like Lethabo, budgeting is essential for avoiding debt and reducing financial stress.

Step 1: Calculate Your Income

The first step in creating a budget is knowing how much money you have coming in. For most students, income comes from a combination of student loans, part-time jobs, scholarships, and financial aid. Be sure to include all sources of income, no matter how small. Don't forget about side gigs like tutoring or freelance work. Knowing your total monthly income gives you a clearer picture of what you can afford to spend.

Step 2: List Your Expenses

Next, it's time to track your spending. Start by listing all your fixed expenses—rent, tuition, transportation, and essentials like water and electricity. Then, move on to variable expenses like groceries, entertainment, and social outings. It's easy to forget about smaller, everyday purchases like coffee, snacks, or takeaways, which can add up quickly.

Being honest about your spending habits is important. If you tend to overspend on food, clothing, or social activities, it's vital to acknowledge it. The goal is to track every rand and identify areas where you can cut back.

Step 3: Allocate Savings

Even as a learner or student, saving money is important. While it may not be possible to save large amounts, setting aside even a small percentage of your income can help you build a financial cushion. A good rule of thumb is to aim to save at least 10% of your income, no matter how little it may seem. This can help you avoid falling into the trap of living paycheck to paycheck.

By making savings a priority, you can create an emergency fund that will help you weather unexpected financial challenges, like medical expenses or fees you didn't plan for.

Tools to Help You Budget:

There are several budgeting apps and tools that can make tracking your finances easier:

- **YNAB (You Need A Budget)** - A popular student app that helps you plan how to spend your money, set savings, and keep track of different spending categories.

- **Mint** - A free app that automatically syncs with your bank accounts and tracks your spending.

- **GoodBudget** - A simple app that lets you divide your money into different "envelopes" – like transport, food, or data – so you can stick to your budget and avoid overspending.

If you prefer a more hands-on approach, you can also create a budget template using a spreadsheet program like Google Sheets or Microsoft Excel. There are also many pre-made templates available online.

Interactive Element:

Here's a simple exercise to get you started:

Create Your Budget Template

1. List your income and expenses for the month.

2. Create two columns: one for income and one for expenses.

3. Subtract your expenses from your income to see if you have any money left over.

4. Consider how much you can set aside for savings.

Here's an example of a real student's budget:

Student Budget Template

Name: Tando

Month: March 2025

Income:

Source of Income	Amount (ZAR)
Part-time job (Retail)	3,000
Scholarship	1,500
Family allowance	1,000
Total Income	5,500

Expenses:

Category	Amount (ZAR)
Rent	1,800
Groceries	1,000
Transportation (Bus/Taxi)	400
Study Materials (Books, etc.)	300
Phone & Internet	300

Category	Amount (ZAR)
Entertainment & Socializing	500
Other	200
Total Expenses	**4,500**

Balance Calculation:

- **Income**: 5,500 ZAR

- **Expenses**: 4,500 ZAR

- **Remaining Balance**: 5,500 - 4,500 = **1,000 ZAR**

Savings Consideration:

- **Amount to Set Aside for Savings**: 500 ZAR

- **Remaining for Spending**: 500 ZAR

Reflection:

Tando has a positive balance of 1,000 ZAR after covering all expenses. He decided to save 500 ZAR, leaving another 500 ZAR for additional spending or emergencies. By tracking income and expenses, Tando can stay within budget and prioritize savings for future goals, such as study-related costs or emergencies.

By doing this exercise, you'll have a clear visual of your finances and can adjust your spending habits accordingly.

Smart Saving Strategies

Saving money isn't just for wealthy people—it's for anyone who wants to build financial stability, no matter their income. In fact, having a small emergency fund can make a huge difference when life throws unexpected expenses your way.

The Benefits of Saving: Having money saved up gives you peace of mind. It acts as a financial safety net, offering security and independence when life doesn't go according to plan. Whether it's dealing with an unexpected medical bill, fixing a broken laptop, or covering unexpected travel costs, having an emergency fund can help you stay calm in challenging situations. Plus, cultivating a savings habit early in life sets you up for long-term financial stability.

Practical Tips for Saving:

- **Open a Savings Account**: If you don't already have one, consider opening a separate savings account. This account should be for emergencies, making it harder to access impulsively. By keeping your savings apart from your everyday spending, you're less likely to dip into it.

- **Automate Your Savings**: One of the easiest ways to save is by setting up automatic transfers from your checking account to your savings account each month. Even if it's just a small amount, automating ensures you're consistently saving without thinking about it.

- **Cut Unnecessary Expenses**: Take a close look at your spending habits. Are you buying coffee every day? Do you have subscriptions you rarely use? By cutting back on small, non-essential purchases, you'll be surprised how quickly you can save.

Enhancement Tip: Remember, saving doesn't always have to be about big amounts. For example, if you cut out buying coffee every day, you could save around 20-30 rands a month. These small amounts quickly accumulate. After a few months, that could be enough to cover an unexpected emergency or even add to your larger savings goals.

Avoiding the Debt Trap

Debt can feel like a never-ending spiral, but it doesn't have to be. Lethabo found herself overwhelmed by mounting bills, credit card debt, and loans that felt impossible to pay off. The freedom of using credit cards and payday loans quickly turned into a trap—what started as a small, innocent purchase spiraled into unnecessary debt. The emotional toll of this debt weighed heavily on her, making it difficult to focus on her studies and the future she dreamed of.

Risks of Debt:

- **Credit Cards** - They offer immediate access to funds, but the interest rates and fees can make repayment difficult.

- **Payday Loans** - These may seem like a quick fix, but they often trap you in a cycle of high-interest debt.

- **Overspending**: It's easy to justify purchases, but over time, this can add up and result in overwhelming debt.

Solutions to Avoid Debt:

- **Responsible Borrowing** - Only borrow when absolutely necessary, and make sure you can afford the repayments.

- **Seek Financial Aid** - Don't hesitate to apply for scholarships, bursaries, or financial support to help with tuition and living expenses.

- **Part-Time Work** - Earning money through a part-time job can ease financial pressure and prevent you from relying on debt.

Reflection Prompt:

- What are some ways you can avoid falling into debt? Write down at least two strategies you can start using today to control your spending.

- Think of a time when you made a purchase you later regretted. What could you have done differently?

- How can you create a budget that reflects your values and helps you avoid financial stress?

Income Generation: Earning While Learning

Lethabo knew that relying solely on her student allowance wouldn't give her the financial freedom she desired. She began exploring ways to earn money without sacrificing her academic goals. Her journey led her to part-time jobs, freelancing, and entrepreneurial ventures, all of which helped her gain both income and valuable skills.

Opportunities to Earn While Studying:

- **Part-Time Jobs** - Many students find success in part-time work that fits around their class schedule. Jobs on campus or in retail are popular options.

- **Freelancing** - If you have a skill—whether it's writing, graphic design, or tutoring—freelancing is a great way to earn. Lethabo, for example, started offering tutoring services to high school students struggling with English. It gave her flexibility and allowed her to earn while helping others.

- **Small Businesses** - Lethabo also turned a hobby into a business, starting an online jewelry store. Her small side hustle not only brought in money but also introduced her to entrepreneurship. The skills she learned, like online marketing and customer service, would benefit her for years to come.

Enhancement Tip: Many students around the world have successfully turned their hobbies into profitable ventures. For example, Monica, a student from Johannesburg, loved photography and spent her weekends capturing moments at events and gatherings. She started sharing her work on social media, and soon, friends and family began hiring her for their own events. What started as a hobby soon blossomed into a full-time photography business. Another student, Toby, turned his love for baking into a small business, creating custom cakes for birthdays and weddings. With hard work and dedication, both Lethabo and Thabo found financial success by doing what they loved.

What's something you love doing that could turn into a source of income?

Scholarships and Financial Aid

Paying for college or university can be expensive, but Lethabo quickly discovered that there were a multitude of financial resources available to help students like her. Scholarships and financial aid aren't just for students with the highest grades—they're available to students from all backgrounds and disciplines.

Types of Financial Aid:

- **Merit-Based Scholarships** - Awarded based on academic achievements, leadership, or other talents.

- **Need-Based Scholarships** - For students who demonstrate financial need.

- **Field-Specific Scholarships** - Scholarships tailored to students pursuing particular fields of study, like engineering, arts, or education.

Steps to Apply for Scholarships:

1. **Research**: Find scholarships that match your academic interests, financial situation, and background.

2. **Prepare Documentation**: Ensure you have all necessary documents, such as transcripts, proof of income, and letters of recommendation.

3. **Apply**: Follow the scholarship application instructions carefully and submit all materials before the deadline.

4. **Follow-up**: Make sure your application was received, and check back if you haven't heard anything after a while.

Enhancement Tip:

- **South African Scholarships:**

- o **NSFAS (National Student Financial Aid Scheme)** – Offers financial aid for eligible South African students.

- o **Funza Lushaka Bursary Scheme** – Provides bursaries for students pursuing teaching careers.

- o **Government Scholarships** – These include opportunities like the Chevening and Commonwealth scholarships.

- **Global Scholarships:**

  - o Chevening Scholarships – Study in the UK.

  - o **Fulbright Program** – Study in the United States.

  - o **Commonwealth Scholarships** – For students in member countries.

By seeking out these financial resources, you can ease the financial burden of your studies and focus more on learning and growing.

Financial Tools and Resources

Managing money isn't something you learn overnight, and it's not just about budgeting. It's about using the right tools to keep track of your spending, saving, and long-term financial planning. Just like how Lethabo discovered, leveraging apps, books, and financial services can make the process of managing your money smoother and more efficient.

Tools to Assist with Financial Management

- **YNAB (You Need A Budget):** A powerful tool for budgeting that helps you prioritize your spending and track your progress toward savings goals. It's especially useful for students who need a structured way to manage limited funds.

- **Mint:** A free app that connects directly to your bank account, automatically tracking all your spending and categorizing it for you. Mint also helps you set up financial goals and alerts to ensure you're sticking to your budget.

- **Local South African Tools:**
- **MoneySmart:** A tool designed specifically for South African students, helping you manage your budget, track your expenses, and save money.
- **Budget Tracker:** Another excellent app for keeping track of where your money is going and setting realistic financial goals.

Books and Websites on Financial Literacy

To fully understand how to handle your finances, it helps to educate yourself with trusted financial resources. Here are a few that can guide you on your financial journey:

- **The Total Money Makeover by Dave Ramsey** - A straightforward guide to taking control of your finances, paying off debt, and building savings.
- **Smart About Money** - An online resource that provides practical tips for managing your finances effectively, with an emphasis on students.
- **My Money South Africa** - This website is tailored to South African residents and offers tools, calculators, and articles to help you make informed decisions about your finances.

Support Services

Universities and colleges often offer free resources for students who need help managing their finances. Look out for:

- **Financial Counseling:** Many universities and colleges have on-campus advisors who can help you create a financial plan, set budgets, and explore options like student loans or scholarships.

- **Workshops:** Workshops on budgeting, saving, and managing student loans can be invaluable in giving you the tools you need to succeed.

- **One-on-One Sessions:** Talking to a financial advisor about your specific needs and goals can help set you on the right path toward long-term financial health.

Interactive Element:

Take a moment to explore one financial tool that could help you manage your finances better. Whether it's an app, book, or website, research, and list at least one financial tool you plan to start using today.

Reflections and Takeaways

By now, you've learned valuable lessons on managing your finances. At times, it may feel overwhelming, especially with the pressures of college or university life and the balancing act of assignments, social events, and limited income. But, just like Lethabo, developing good financial habits now will shape the way you handle money throughout your life.

The key takeaway here is that the skills you've learned, like budgeting, saving, and controlling your spending, are the foundation of financial independence. These lessons will serve you not just in college or university but throughout adulthood.

Think about it like this: You wouldn't expect to run a marathon without preparation and practice. Similarly, achieving financial independence requires careful planning, smart decisions, and—most importantly—consistent effort. Each time you choose to save instead of spend or resist that impulse purchase, you are building the foundation of your financial future. These small decisions, while seemingly insignificant, compound over time and contribute to long-term success.

- Reflect on your financial journey so far.

- Have you been able to stick to your budget?

- Have you made strides in saving, even if it's just a small amount each month?

- Remember, no step is too small when it comes to building a solid financial future.

Building Your Financial Future

It may feel like your financial goals are far out of reach, but remember: Financial success doesn't happen overnight. It's built on steady, consistent actions. Just like a garden, your financial future thrives on small but consistent steps—watering the seeds of savings, budgeting, and discipline will eventually yield the fruits of financial independence.

The most important thing is to start now.

Start by creating a budget, saving, and becoming mindful of where your money is going. Even small changes, made regularly, will lead to significant improvements over time. Financial freedom isn't about making grand gestures or instant success; it's about making small, wise decisions that accumulate into long-term stability.

Each time you choose to save instead of spend, each time you track your expenses or resist an impulse purchase, you are taking control of your financial future. Awareness is the first step toward financial independence, and as you take these small, deliberate steps, you'll notice that your financial journey is not a sprint—it's a marathon, and you've already taken the first step.

Motivational Quote:

"Financial independence begins with awareness and small, steady steps."

Chapter 9:

The Power of Community

The Group That Changed Everything

A Story of Strength and Support

Thobi sat in a crowded university library, surrounded by the quiet hum of students absorbed in their books. Just a few months ago, she had felt completely alone, struggling to keep up with her coursework and battling self-doubt. But today, as she exchanged notes with her study group, she realized something profound, she wasn't alone.

The group had formed organically, starting with casual conversations in class. Over time, they became a lifeline for each other, providing not only academic support but also emotional encouragement. They celebrated each other's victories, consoled one another through failures, and pushed each other to do better. It wasn't just about studying anymore; it was about belonging.

Thobi's story is not unique. Many students navigate the complexities of college and university life feeling isolated, but the right community can transform their experience. Whether it's a study group, a club, or a close-knit circle of friends, a strong support system can provide the strength needed to face challenges and succeed.

The Power of Community: My Story

Raised by a Village

Thobi was raised by a single mother, a dedicated primary school teacher and her paternal grandparents. Together, they provided the love, guidance, and unwavering support that shaped her early life. Though her grandmother passed away when Thobi was just seven, the values she embodied remained vivid in Thobi's memory. She instilled in her a strong sense of self-assertion, confidence, and purpose.

Her grandfather, despite never having learned to read or write, taught her the importance of hard work, perseverance, and resilience. Born in 1924, he held progressive views that defied traditional gender roles. He believed every person, regardless of gender, deserved the chance to pursue their dreams.

As a child, Thobi often accompanied her grandfather on weekend construction jobs. He never treated her as too young or too weak to learn. Instead, he taught her practical skills, independence, and self-reliance, lessons that would shape her outlook and determination for years to come.

Breaking Gender Stereotypes

Thobi's mother and grandfather helped shape her belief that gender roles are socially constructed. She learned early on that hard work and determination are not limited by gender. Their teachings became the foundation of her educational journey, career path, and personal growth.

Later in life, her husband became one of her strongest supporters, sharing parenting responsibilities and encouraging her professional aspirations. Together, they built a partnership rooted in mutual respect and a shared belief that success is a collaborative journey.

For her children, nieces, and nephews, Thobi consistently emphasized the value of hard work and resilience. She wanted them to grow up believing that nothing is impossible when approached with discipline and determination.

The Power of Mentors

In high school, Thobi was introduced to three principles that changed the trajectory of her life:

- Discipline

- Commitment

- Excellence

These values were deeply reinforced by two important figures: her late netball coach and her high school principal. Her coach reminded students that their health, time, and dedication mattered—not just in sports but in all aspects of life. Her principal encouraged preparation for the unexpected, emphasizing the importance of staying ahead in studies and developing lifelong habits.

These lessons proved invaluable when, just before her final exams, Thobi fell seriously ill. With limited time to prepare, she relied on the Saturday study sessions she once saw as optional. Those sessions made all the difference.

She passed. She made it to university.

In that moment, Thobi understood the impact of discipline, preparation, and the strength of a community that believed in her. Defining Community in College/University Life

What Does Community Mean for Students?

Community, in the context of higher education, is more than just a collection of individuals. It is a dynamic support network that can shape a student's academic, emotional, and professional development. For many students, different types of communities contribute to growth and overall well-being during their time at college or university.

Types of Student Communities:

- Academic Communities – These include study groups, research teams, and academic societies that offer intellectual engagement and academic assistance.

- Social Communities – Formed through friendships, student organizations, and sports teams, these groups provide emotional support and help build meaningful relationships.

- Advocacy Communities – These are focused on driving social change, promoting inclusion, and supporting causes important to students and their peers.

Benefits of Belonging to a Community:

- Emotional Support – A sense of belonging reduces stress and boosts resilience.

- Shared Learning – Collaborating with peers enhances academic understanding and encourages knowledge exchange.

- Networking Opportunities – Student communities can lead to mentorships, internships, and future job prospects.

Building Your Own Community: A Legacy of Love and Support

The Foundation of Strong Communities

Strong communities don't arise by chance, they are intentionally built on shared values, mutual respect, and a collective commitment to uplift one another. Whether within academic environments, social groups, or professional networks, the most impactful communities are those that promote growth, inclusivity, and a sense of purpose.

At the heart of any meaningful community lies a central question: What legacy will be left behind?

For Thobi, the answer has always been consistent, a legacy rooted in love, healing, and empowerment.

Influenced by the lessons instilled by her grandparents and the unwavering guidance of her mentors, Thobi came to understand that building a true community means sharing wisdom, offering support, and creating spaces where others are empowered to thrive.

Steps to Building a Supportive Community

Whether you're looking to create a study group, a club, or a professional network, the key to success lies in intentionality and inclusivity. Here are some steps to help you build a strong and lasting community:

Identify a Shared Goal: What brings people together? Whether it's academic success, a social cause, or career advancement, having a common purpose creates direction and unity.

Foster Inclusivity: A welcoming environment ensures that everyone feels valued. Be open to diverse perspectives and create a space where all voices are heard.

Encourage Collaboration: No one thrives in isolation. Ensure that everyone contributes and has a role in shaping the community's success.

Resolve Conflicts with Respect: Disagreements are natural, but handling them with patience and empathy is key. Establish clear communication and address conflicts constructively.

Pass It On: True leadership is about creating opportunities for others. Think about what values and lessons you want to pass on and ensure your community continues to uplift future members.

Checklist: Steps to Start a Peer Study Group or Club

- Define your mission and purpose.

- Find like-minded individuals who share your vision.

- Establish roles and responsibilities.

- Set clear expectations for participation and collaboration.

- Maintain regular communication and meetings.

- Create a supportive and inclusive environment.

- Plan for sustainability—who will carry the community forward?

Reflection Prompt:

- What values do you hope to pass on to this world or your loved ones?

- How can you create a supportive and lasting community in your academic, personal, or professional life?

Mentorship and Role Models: Learning from Those Who Came Before Us

The Transformative Power of Mentorship

Throughout my life, I have been fortunate to walk alongside mentors who shaped my journey. From my grandparents and teachers to my professional mentors, each played a role in guiding me toward success.

Mentorship is one of the most powerful forms of support a person can receive. Whether it's helping navigate academic challenges, offering career advice, or providing emotional encouragement, a mentor can be the difference between giving up and pushing forward.

The Power of Mentorship: Unlocking Hidden Potential

As I reflect on my journey, I realize that people who had a strong influence in shaping my professional development and personal growth. Sir Emma Belot and Malik Jaffer seasoned public health professionals who took me under their wings and became my mentors.

I met Emma while doing my postgraduate degree in psychology, when I was struggling to find footing, onto my second degree and with minimal prospects of employment opportunities. She was then training manager, and I was just a young graduate trying to navigate the corporate world. Our paths crossed during my practical work, and she took notice of my eagerness to learn and grow. Her mentorship was not limited to our formal meetings. She would often call me to discuss industry trends, share her experiences, and offer valuable advice. Her guidance helped me to develop a growth mindset, and I began to see challenges as opportunities for progress rather than threats to my ego.

Malik Jaffer created an enabling environment for me to grow and seek identified opportunities for my professional development. Through his support and mentorship, I gained a deeper understanding of myself and began to take advantage of my strengths to achieve my goals.

His mentorship also helped me to develop a sense of purpose and direction. He encouraged me to explore different areas of technical responsibilities, network with colleagues, and seek out new challenges. He sent me to several training development programs, amongst them Harvard School of Public Health for various public health programs. As I gained more experience and confidence, I began to see myself as a leader and started to pursue prospects that fit with my values and passions.

Looking back, I realize that they were not just about helping me to achieve my career goals. They also assisted me in discovering my potential, building my confidence, and developing a growth mindset. Their guidance and support helped me to unlock a part of myself I never knew existed. As I navigated the ups and downs of my career, they were always there to offer guidance and support. They celebrated my successes and helped me learn from my failures. Their mentorship was a constant source of inspiration and motivation, and it helped me stay focused on my goals even when the journey got tough.

As you read this chapter, I encourage you to reflect on the mentors in your life. Who are the people who have helped you to grow and develop as a person? What lessons have you learned from them, and how have they impacted your life?

Remember, mentorship is a two-way street. It requires effort and commitment from both the mentor and the mentee. If you're looking for a mentor, don't be afraid to reach out to someone you admire or respect. And if you're already in a mentorship relationship, make sure to appreciate and value the guidance and support you're receiving.

How to Identify and Approach a Mentor

Finding the right mentor can seem overwhelming, but the process is simpler than it looks. Here are a few steps:

Look for Role Models in Your Field: Who inspires you? This could be a professor, a senior student, a professional, or even an online mentor whose work you admire.

Be Open to Learning: A mentorship relationship is a two-way street. Approach it with curiosity, humility, and a willingness to grow.

Seek Guidance with Clarity: When reaching out to a mentor, be specific about what you need help with—whether it's advice on a career path, study strategies, or professional networking.

Build Genuine Connections: Mentorship is not just about receiving; it's also about appreciating and learning from the mentor's experiences. Express gratitude and stay engaged.

Sidebar: Tips for Building a Strong Mentorship Relationship

Set Clear Goals: Define what you hope to gain from the mentorship.

Communicate Regularly: Stay in touch, whether through in-person meetings, emails, or calls, and respect their time.

Be Open to Feedback: Constructive criticism is an opportunity for growth.

Give Back: As you grow, mentor someone else—pass on the wisdom you receive.

Reflection Prompt:

- Who has been a mentor in your life, and how have they impacted you?

- What steps can you take to seek out a mentor who fits with your goals?

Collaborative Learning: The Power of Teamwork

Why Collaboration Matters

Education is often viewed as an individual pursuit, but the truth is that learning is most effective when it happens together.

When students collaborate, they gain:

Diverse Perspectives: Different backgrounds lead to new ideas and deeper insights.

Shared Accountability: Working with others keeps you motivated and committed to your goals.

Stronger Problem-Solving Skills: Tackling challenges as a group helps develop critical thinking and adaptability.

How to Foster Collaborative Learning

Here are some strategies for effective collaboration in academic and professional settings:

Define Goals Clearly: Before starting a group project or study session, ensure everyone understands the objectives.

Respect Individual Strengths: Each person brings unique skills—some excel at research, while others are great at organizing or presenting. Recognize and use these strengths.

Encourage Active Participation: Make sure everyone contributes and feels valued. A strong community thrives on mutual effort.

Establish Ground Rules: To avoid conflicts, set expectations early—such as respecting deadlines, being open to different viewpoints, and maintaining open communication.

Seek Out New Learning Partners: Don't just limit yourself to one group—join different study circles, work together with people from different subjects or fields, and expand your circle of connections.

Exercise: List Potential Classmates to Work With

Take a moment to reflect on your current academic circle.

- Who in your class or campus shares your drive for success?

- Are there students you admire for their dedication and work ethic?

- How can you actively work together with them?

Final Thoughts: The Strength in Community

Whether it's through peer study groups, mentorship, or teamwork, your community will not only shape your academic journey but your personal and professional growth as well.

The relationships you nurture today are a foundation for lifelong learning and success.

As you move forward, remember:

Build a community that reflects your values.

Seek and become a mentor.

Learn, grow, and support others along the way.

No one succeeds alone. The strongest people are those who lift others up.

Diversity and Inclusion in Communities

The Strength in Differences

A truly thriving community is one that embraces diversity and encourages inclusivity. Whether in an academic setting, a workplace, or a social group, diverse perspectives enhance learning, innovation, and understanding.

South Africa is a richly diverse country—culturally, racially, linguistically, and socioeconomically. However, diversity alone isn't enough; we must also create inclusive spaces where everyone feels valued and respected.

Why Diversity Matters

Enhances Learning and Growth: Exposure to different perspectives challenges biases and broadens thinking.

Encourages Working Together: Inclusive communities create environments where all voices are heard and contributions are valued.

Promotes Social Awareness: Engaging with people from different backgrounds builds empathy and deepens cultural understanding.

Addressing Biases and Breaking Barriers

Despite the benefits of diversity, exclusion and discrimination can still occur. Whether based on gender, race, religion, disability, or sexual orientation, biases create barriers that prevent full participation in communities.

To combat these issues, we must:

Recognize Our Own Biases: Challenge stereotypes and question preconceived notions.

Encourage Open Conversations: Create spaces where people feel safe discussing their identities and experiences.

Advocate for Inclusivity: Speak up when exclusion or discrimination occurs.

Success Stories from South African Campuses

Many universities and colleges in South Africa are taking bold steps to foster inclusivity.

University of Cape Town's Inclusivity Drive: The University has implemented a disability-friendly infrastructure, gender-neutral restrooms, and diversity awareness programs to ensure that students from all backgrounds feel welcome.

False Bay TVET College's Accessible Learning Model: Known for its strong commitment to inclusivity, False Bay TVET College offers assistive learning technologies, campus accessibility improvements, and student support services tailored for individuals with disabilities.

To support broader transformation, several national initiatives are also driving change:

- **Higher Education Disability Services Association (HEDSA):** Enhances disability inclusion in the post-school education and training sector through online tools, resource sharing, and institutional collaboration.

- **The Education Plus Initiative:** A regional advocacy campaign aimed at expanding access to secondary education in Sub-Saharan Africa, especially for adolescent girls and young women, while promoting health, education, and human rights.

Reflection Prompt:

- What does inclusivity mean to you?

- Have you ever witnessed or experienced exclusion? How can you help create a more inclusive community in your academic or personal life?

The Role of Digital Communities

The Digital World as a Community Builder

With the rise of technology, communities are no longer confined to physical spaces. Digital platforms have made it easier than ever to connect, learn, and work together—whether through academic forums, social media, or professional networks.

Benefits of Digital Communities

Accessibility & Global Reach: Digital platforms break geographical barriers, allowing students from different parts of the world to share knowledge and experiences.

Support Networks: Online communities provide safe spaces for individuals to find like-minded people, especially for those who feel isolated in their immediate surroundings.

Endless Learning Opportunities: Through webinars, online courses, and virtual mentorship programs, students can enhance their knowledge and skills beyond the classroom.

Challenges and Risks of Online Communities

Despite their many advantages, digital spaces also present unique challenges:

Misinformation: The internet is flooded with false or misleading information—always verify sources before accepting something as fact.

Cyberbullying & Toxicity: Online spaces can become hostile, with harassment and bullying making some communities unsafe.

Privacy & Security Concerns: Personal data shared online can be exploited—it's important to protect your information and engage safely.

How to Foster Positive Digital Interactions

Engage Respectfully: Treat online conversations with the same respect as in-person discussions.

Verify Information Before Sharing: Always fact-check to avoid spreading misinformation.

Be Selective with Your Digital Communities: Surround yourself with uplifting and empowering online networks that fit with your personal and academic goals.

Block and Report Toxic Behavior: If you witness cyberbullying, harassment, or discrimination, take action by reporting the behavior.

Journal Prompt:

- How can digital platforms complement your community goals?

- Have you found an online space that has positively impacted your academic or personal growth?

Final Thoughts: Building Bridges in All Spaces

Whether through face-to-face interactions or digital platforms, the strength of any community lies in how well it embraces diversity, supports its members, and fosters meaningful connections.

As you navigate your academic and personal journey, remember to choose and build communities that inspire growth, encourage inclusivity, and provide a sense of belonging.

Your community is your support system—build it wisely.

Reflections and Takeaways

The Lessons of Community

Throughout this chapter, we have explored the significance of building, nurturing, and participating in communities that foster personal and academic success. Whether through mentorship, peer collaboration, inclusivity, or digital networks, the communities we engage with shape our growth, offer support, and expand our opportunities.

Key Takeaways

Community-Building Fosters Growth

A strong community not only provides emotional support but also enhances academic performance, career development, and personal well-being.

Diversity Enriches Experiences

When we embrace diversity in our communities, we gain new perspectives, challenge biases, and become more open-minded.

Mentorship and Collaboration Unlock Potential

Learning from others—whether through mentorship or peer collaboration—accelerates personal and academic development.

The Power of Digital Connections

Online platforms can amplify opportunities, help students find like-minded people, and provide access to resources beyond geographical limits.

Reflection Prompt:

- What steps can you take to build a meaningful community this year?

- Consider both in-person and digital spaces—how can you engage with them to grow academically and personally?

Strength in Togetherness

The Role of Community in Resilience and Success

No one succeeds alone. Every great achievement is supported by a network of people who offer encouragement, knowledge, and opportunities.

As you step forward in your academic and personal journey, choose your communities wisely. Surround yourself with people who uplift, challenge, and inspire you. Be open to learning from those with different backgrounds and experiences. Most importantly, give back—contribute to your community in ways that make it stronger for others.

The Call to Action: Seek and Build Your Community

Join study groups, mentorship programs, or networking communities.

Seek out diverse perspectives and advocate for inclusivity.

Offer support and encouragement to others on their journey.

Use digital platforms to enhance your learning and career prospects.

Final Thought

The strength of community is not just in what we receive but in what we give. Be intentional in building, contributing to, and uplifting the communities around you—because success is always greater when shared.

Motivational Quote:

"Alone we can do so little; together we can do so much."

– Helen Keller.

Chapter 10:

The Entrepreneurial Mindset

The Side Hustle That Paid Tuition

Sipho is a second-year student at university, juggling the demanding requirements of his studies with a growing side hustle. He isn't just a student; he is a self-made entrepreneur. With a good eye for fashion and an understanding of what his peers wanted, Sipho started selling trendy clothing items—swag tops, T-shirts, caps, and jeans. These were affordable yet stylish pieces that resonated with the student body.

However, Sipho's journey wasn't without its challenges. Finding quality materials within a tight budget, dealing with suppliers, and figuring out how to market his products without a large advertising budget were just a few of the hurdles he faced. On top of that, balancing his academic responsibilities with his business was not easy at all. Yet, Sipho didn't give up.

Through determination, creativity, and hard work, Sipho's side hustle grew to the point where he was paying his tuition fees and more. His business not only helped him achieve financial independence but also allowed him to develop valuable skills like marketing, inventory management, and customer relations—skills that would serve him well in his future career.

Sipho's story is one of resilience and vision. He saw a problem—students needing affordable, stylish clothes—and found a way to solve it. His entrepreneurial journey is a perfect example of how, with the right mindset, any student can turn challenges into opportunities.

What is an Entrepreneurial Mindset?

An entrepreneurial mindset is more than just the desire to start a business. It's a way of thinking and approaching problems. It's about being creative, adaptable, and resilient in the face of challenges. Whether or not you plan to start your own business, adopting an entrepreneurial mindset can be beneficial in any field or aspect of life.

Core Traits of an Entrepreneurial Mindset:

- **Creativity:** Entrepreneurs often think outside the box. They come up with innovative solutions to problems and seek new ways to approach tasks.

- **Adaptability:** Being able to adjust when things don't go as planned is a key part of success. Entrepreneurs are flexible and can navigate uncertainty.

- **Resilience:** Setbacks are a part of any journey, but resilience is about bouncing back and continuing to move forward. Entrepreneurs embrace failure as a learning experience.

- **Curiosity:** Entrepreneurs are always asking questions, seeking new knowledge, and exploring opportunities. They stay curious about the world around them and look for ways to improve.

Entrepreneurship: More Than Just Starting a Business

While starting a business is a key aspect of entrepreneurship, the entrepreneurial mindset can also be applied in any situation. Whether it's solving a problem at school, improving a process at work, or coming up with a creative solution to a challenge, entrepreneurial thinking is about applying these core traits to create positive change.

Entrepreneurial thinking can help you take control and turn obstacles into stepping stones.

Reflection Prompt:

- Reflect on an area in your life where you're facing challenges.

- How can adopting an entrepreneurial mindset help you overcome these challenges?

- Think about how creativity, risk-taking, and problem-solving could create new opportunities.

- Can you approach the issue from a fresh perspective or find innovative solutions?

- Identify one way you can apply entrepreneurial thinking to your personal goals.

Identifying Opportunities

A key part of developing an entrepreneurial mindset is learning how to spot opportunities. Opportunities are everywhere if you know where to look. Often, they come from recognizing unmet needs or gaps in a market or identifying ways to improve an existing product or service.

Sipho, for example, identified an opportunity in the clothing market on his campus. While students wanted affordable and stylish clothing, the options available were often either too expensive or not trendy enough. By noticing this gap, Sipho saw an opportunity to create something that appealed to his peers while fitting within their budget.

The Reality of South Africa's Youth Employment

The transition from college or university to the workforce is often filled with uncertainty. Many graduates struggle to secure jobs, not because of a lack of ambition or effort but because employers believe they lack the practical skills needed for entry-level roles. This reality places immense pressure on young people, who are often left wondering if their education has adequately prepared them for the challenges ahead.

Currently, South Africa's youth unemployment rate stands at 46.6% (QLFS Q3, 2024). This means that almost half of the youth population is unable to get jobs. Even more alarming, 3.5 million young people aged 15-24 years are not in employment, education, or training (NEET). Among these groups, young black women are hit the hardest, often finding it difficult to access opportunities because of economic and social challenges.

The reasons for these challenges include:

- **Skills mismatch:** Many graduates enter the job market without the necessary technical, practical, or soft skills employers demand. They might know the theory, but without real-world experience, they're at a disadvantage.

- **Limited work-integrated learning:** Unlike developed countries where internships and apprenticeships are compulsory, many South African students graduate without ever having set foot in a professional work environment. This gap in experience often leads employers to favor those who've already worked in the industry.

- **Barriers to inclusion:** Young people from underrepresented communities, rural backgrounds, and the LGBTQI+ community face additional hurdles in getting jobs. Unfair systems and hidden biases often lead to fewer opportunities and make it harder to grow in a career.

- **Unequal access to information:** Many job seekers are unaware of available opportunities, funding programs, and skill development initiatives simply because this information is not easily accessible to them.

- **Poorly run public employment programs**: While there are initiatives to support youth employment, they are often poorly implemented, underfunded, or difficult to navigate.

The Solution: Thinking Beyond Traditional Employment

Given these challenges, young people must start thinking beyond traditional employment and embrace an entrepreneurial mindset. Developing entrepreneurial thinking allows students to:

Create their own opportunities instead of waiting for job offers.

Develop skills that make them more employable and adaptable to market changes.

Start small businesses or side hustles that can provide financial independence.

Find innovative ways to solve local problems, building careers that benefit communities.

The future belongs to those who are proactive, innovative, and willing to take risks. If traditional employment structures don't accommodate young job seekers, then entrepreneurship provides a valuable alternative path to success.

Steps to Identifying Opportunities:

1. **Look for Unmet Needs:** Pay attention to the problems or needs that others have. What are people struggling with or complaining about? Is there a way you can provide a solution?

2. **Research and Validate:** Once you've identified an opportunity, do some research. Ask your peers, conduct surveys, or look for trends to see if your idea can work. Validating your idea ensures that there is demand and interest in what you want to offer.

3. **Think Locally:** Opportunities don't always need to be big or global. Sometimes, the best ideas come from solving small, local

problems. Whether it's a gap in campus services, a need for better study tools, or an overlooked local need, small ideas can grow into great business opportunities.

4. **Use Available Tools and Support:** Don't overlook the resources available to you. Whether it's access to university or college networks, online platforms, or the support of friends and family, make use of the tools at your disposal.

Example:

Sipho didn't start with a huge budget or a big marketing campaign. He used word-of-mouth social media and worked together with local influencers to promote his clothing line. His ability to see the potential in everyday opportunities helped him grow his business.

Next Steps: Applying Entrepreneurial Thinking

Now that you understand what an entrepreneurial mindset is and how to spot opportunities, it's time to think about how you can apply this mindset in your own life.

1. **Think About a Problem You Encounter Regularly:** This could be in your academic life, your personal life, or even in your community. What frustrates you or others? Could you find a way to fix it or make it better?

2. **Start Small:** You don't have to launch a large-scale business to apply an entrepreneurial mindset. Start by taking on small projects or by offering solutions to small problems in your day-to-day life.

3. **Take Risks:** Entrepreneurship requires taking risks. It's important to take calculated risks that fit with your goals but don't be afraid to step out of your comfort zone and try new things.

4. **Learn from Failure:** Not every idea will be successful, and that's okay. The important thing is to learn from failure, adapt, and keep moving forward.

Overcoming Fear and Failure

Failure is a part of any journey, especially in the world of entrepreneurship. Many successful entrepreneurs have faced setbacks, but their ability to learn from those experiences has been key to their success. Failure isn't something to be feared—it's a powerful tool for growth.

Famous Entrepreneurs Who Failed Before They Succeeded:

- **Richard Maponya – Building a Business Empire Against All Odds**

  Richard Maponya always believed in creating something bigger – but growing up during apartheid meant he faced serious limitations. He was denied a license to open a clothing store in a white area, even though he had a strong business plan. Instead of giving up, he started small: selling clothes and milk in Black communities, often working out of his car.

  Over time, he built a business empire – from retail to real estate – always focused on serving his community. He eventually opened *Maponya Mall* in Soweto, one of the largest malls in South Africa.

  Lesson: Even when the system is against you, determination and vision can take you far. If you don't go through the front door, find another way in.

- **Anda Maqanda – From Failure to a Thriving Tech Business**

  Anda studied electrical engineering but failed his first year. Instead of giving up, he took a break, refocused, and later started his own tech company, AM Group. Today, he's a successful entrepreneur providing engineering and technology solutions.

Lesson: Failing once doesn't mean you're a failure. What matters is how you bounce back.

- **Vusi Thembekwayo – A Bold Voice with Big Dreams**

Vusi started giving public speeches as a teenager and quickly built a name for himself. But not every business idea worked out – he made some risky moves early on that didn't always go as planned. Still, he kept learning, kept building, and became a global business speaker and investor.

Lesson: You don't need to have it all figured out at 18. Start, fail, learn and grow.

- **Sibongile Sambo – Rejected But Not Defeated**

Sibongile always dreamed of working in aviation, but when she was rejected from being a flight attendant, she didn't stop there. Instead, she started her own aviation company – becoming the first Black woman to own one in South Africa.

Lesson: Sometimes rejection is just redirection. When one door closes, build your own runway.

- **Walt Disney – From Rejection to a Global Legacy**

Today, the Disney brand is everywhere – from movies and theme parks to merchandise – but Walt Disney's journey was far from magical at first.

He was once fired from a newspaper job because his editor said he "lacked imagination." His first animation studio went bankrupt. And even *Mickey Mouse* was rejected by several studios before finally getting a chance.

Still, Walt Disney didn't give up. He kept creating, dreaming, and taking risks. Eventually, his belief in storytelling and innovation gave the world characters, films, and experiences that have lasted for generations.

Lesson: Failure doesn't mean you're not good enough – it's often just part of the process. Keep going.

- **Steve Jobs - Failure Was Just the Beginning**

Steve Jobs is known as the visionary behind Apple. But did you know he was once fired from the very company he co-founded?

In the early years of Apple, things didn't always go smoothly. Internal conflicts and business struggles led to Jobs being pushed out. It was a huge blow. But instead of giving up, he used that time to grow up.

He founded a new company (NeXT), bought Pixar (which made Toy Story), and came back to Apple years later – transforming it into one of the most successful companies in the world.

Lesson: Even when doors close, new ones can open – sometimes leading you exactly where you're meant to be.

- **Oprah Winfrey – Turning Pain into Purpose**

Before becoming a global media powerhouse, Oprah Winfrey faced significant personal and professional setbacks. She was born into poverty in rural Mississippi and endured a traumatic childhood marked by abuse and instability. As a young adult, she was fired from her first television job as a news anchor because she was considered "unfit for TV."

But Oprah didn't give up. She used her setbacks as fuel to reinvent herself, eventually creating *The Oprah Winfrey Show* – one of the most influential talk shows in history. Through her empathy, authenticity, and business savvy, she built a media empire and became one of the most powerful women in the world.

Lesson: Failure doesn't define you – resilience, purpose, and belief in your voice do.

These stories show us that failure is often a stepping stone to success. They didn't give up when things didn't go as planned—they learned, adapted, and kept moving forward.

So should you.

Strategies to Overcome Fear of Failure:

1. **Start Small:** Don't expect your first idea to be perfect or your first venture to be a grand success. Starting small helps reduce risk and allows you to learn along the way.

2. **Set Realistic Goals:** Break down big goals into smaller, more manageable steps. This makes it easier to track progress and stay motivated, even when things don't go as planned.

3. **Embrace Setbacks:** View setbacks as lessons, not obstacles. Analyze what went wrong, learn from it, and apply that knowledge to future endeavors.

Motivational Quote:

"Failure is simply the opportunity to begin again, this time more intelligently."

– Henry Ford

Remember, every setback brings new lessons and opportunities for growth. Embrace failure as a natural part of the entrepreneurial process and use it to fuel your drive to succeed.

Facing Workforce Challenges with an Entrepreneurial Spirit

For many young South Africans, the biggest challenge isn't just finding a job – it's breaking through the unfair systems that make it harder for them to succeed at work.

The Reality of Workforce Discrimination

- **LGBTQI+ individuals** often face hiring discrimination, unfair treatment in the workplace, and limited career advancement opportunities. Many struggle to find inclusive work environments where they feel safe and valued.

- **Graduates from disadvantaged backgrounds** often lack professional networks that can provide mentorship and job referrals, making it harder to break into industries dominated by well-connected individuals.

- **Women and young black professionals** still face unequal salaries, underrepresentation in leadership roles, and workplace biases that make it harder for them to grow in their careers.

How an Entrepreneurial Mindset Can Help

When traditional employment avenues fail to provide equal opportunities, an entrepreneurial mindset becomes a powerful tool for empowerment. Instead of passively waiting for opportunities, young people can:

Start a freelance career or small business while applying for jobs—monetize skills like tutoring, photography, design, or writing.

Volunteer or intern to gain experience—show initiative and build skills that make you more employable.

Take advantage of mentorship programs—seek guidance from professionals who can open doors to career opportunities.

Develop a side hustle—many students have successfully built businesses in fashion, e-commerce, digital marketing, and tech services.

Rejection isn't failure—it's redirection. Many successful people, from Oprah Winfrey to Nelson Mandela, faced career setbacks before finding their path. The key is to stay proactive, keep learning, and create opportunities where none seem to exist.

Reflection Prompt:

- Have you ever faced setbacks in job applications or career growth?

- How did you respond to those challenges?

- What skills or strategies can you use to overcome future obstacles?

Balancing Entrepreneurship and Academics

Balancing the demands of academic life and running a business can feel overwhelming at times, but it's not impossible. Many students successfully juggle both and develop valuable skills that benefit them in their academic pursuits and beyond.

Time Management and Organization:

One of the most important skills you need as a student entrepreneur is time management. Between attending classes, completing assignments, and managing your business, staying organized is crucial.

1. **Use a Planner:** Keep track of your assignments, deadlines, and business tasks in one place. This can be a physical planner or a digital tool like Google Calendar or Trello.

2. **Prioritize Tasks:** Understand what needs your attention right away and what can wait. Focus on high-priority tasks first, both for school and your business.

3. **Set Boundaries:** Don't overcommit yourself. Set clear boundaries between academic and business hours so you can give both the time they deserve.

Take Advantage of College or University Resources:

Many colleges and universities offer resources to help student entrepreneurs, such as innovation hubs, business incubators, and student entrepreneurship clubs. Take advantage of these resources to help grow your business while staying focused on your studies.

- **Innovation Hubs:** These centers often provide free access to office space, mentorship, and networking opportunities.

- **Clubs and Competitions:** Join entrepreneurship clubs and participate in business plan competitions to get feedback on your ideas and connect with like-minded students.

Recognizing Limits and Seeking Help:

It's important to recognize when you need help. Don't hesitate to reach out to professors, mentors, or peers for support. Your well-being is important, and sometimes balancing school and business means asking for help when needed.

Interactive Element:

- Plan your ideal week, balancing study and entrepreneurial tasks.

- Create a schedule that includes time for both academic responsibilities and business-related tasks. Be sure to build in time for rest and self-care.

- How can you allocate your time effectively to ensure success in both areas?

Building Skills for Success

Successful entrepreneurs possess a variety of skills, and while some of these can be learned through experience, others can be developed through practice and learning.

The Role of Employability Programs

To close the gap between learning and earning, universities and government agencies have developed employability programs aimed at preparing young graduates for the workforce. These programs include:

Work-Integrated Learning (WIL): Encourages students to gain industry experience through internships, apprenticeships, and cooperative education programs.

Employability Training Programs: Teach essential workplace skills like communication, critical thinking, leadership, and teamwork.

Career Coaching & Mentorship: Connects young job seekers with experienced professionals who provide career guidance and industry insights.

Some of the most impactful South African youth employment programs include:

SAYouth.mobi – A zero-rated platform connecting unemployed youth to job opportunities.

Presidential Youth Employment Intervention (PYEI) – Provides entry-level job placements, entrepreneurship support, and work-based training.

Harambee Youth Employment Accelerator – Bridges the gap between young job seekers and employers by providing training and work-readiness support.

Whether you want to start your own business or secure your first job, investing in skill development is crucial to success.

Key Entrepreneurial Skills:

1. **Communication:**

   o Being able to pitch your ideas effectively is essential. Whether you're seeking investors, collaborating with others, or selling to customers, strong communication skills are critical.

   o Learn to listen and present ideas clearly and confidently. Being able to articulate your vision will help you build credibility and gain support.

2. **Financial Literacy:**

   o Understanding how to manage a budget, track income and expenses, and reinvest profits is key to long-term success.

   o Learn about cash flow management, pricing strategies, and basic accounting practices.

3. **Digital Skills:**

   o In today's digital world, being comfortable with technology is crucial. From using online platforms to market your business to analyzing data for better decision-making, digital skills can help you grow your business.

   o Familiarize yourself with tools like social media management platforms, website builders, and analytics tools.

Enhancement Tip:

Here are some **free online resources** to help you develop these skills:

- **Communication Skills:** Take a course on Coursera or edX on effective communication.

- **Financial Literacy:** Websites like Investopedia and Khan Academy offer free resources on managing money and business finances.

- **Digital Skills:** Platforms like Udemy and Skillshare provide affordable courses on using online tools and building a digital presence.

Creating Value Through Social Entrepreneurship

Entrepreneurship isn't just about making money—it's about creating value and making a positive impact on society. Social entrepreneurship focuses on using business solutions to address pressing social, environmental, or community issues.

Student-Led Ventures Solving Societal Issues:

- **Sustainable Fashion Brands:** Some students are starting clothing lines made from recycled materials or promoting fair-trade practices. This is not just a business—it's a movement to promote sustainability.

- **Social Awareness Campaigns:** Students are also using their entrepreneurial skills to run campaigns that raise awareness about mental health, climate change, or social justice.

Aligning Personal Passions with Societal Needs:

To create a business that has both financial and social impact, align your personal passions with societal needs. What are you passionate about? How can you use that passion to solve a problem in your community or the world?

Reflection Prompt:

- Think about a community issue you care deeply about.

- Is it related to access to education, clean water, or environmental sustainability?

- How does this problem impact the community or individuals?

- If you had the resources, what steps would you take to address it?

- How could entrepreneurship be used as a tool to solve this issue?

- What kind of solutions could you create to make a difference?

- How could you involve others and work together to bring the solution to life?

- What challenges do you anticipate, and how could you overcome them?

Resources and Support Systems

Embarking on an entrepreneurial journey can be daunting, but there are many resources available to help you along the way. Whether you're looking for financial support, mentorship, career guidance, or networking opportunities, you don't have to go it alone.

Campus Resources

Funding Programs – Many universities and colleges offer grants, scholarships, or venture funding programs for student entrepreneurs. These programs provide financial support for innovative business ideas or projects. For example, some South African universities like the University of Cape Town (UCT) and the University of the Witwatersrand (Wits) have dedicated innovation funds to help students get their businesses off the ground.

Mentorship – Universities and colleges often have mentorship programs where students can connect with professors, alumni, and industry professionals who can guide them through their entrepreneurial journey. These mentors provide valuable insights, help navigate challenges, and expand professional networks.

Innovation Hubs – Many universities and colleges now have innovation centers or business incubators, which offer workspace, training, and resources for student entrepreneurs. These hubs provide a collaborative environment where students can brainstorm ideas, build prototypes, and develop their ventures. At institutions like Stellenbosch University, the Stellenbosch University Innovation & Business Hub has played a critical role in supporting student startups.

Online Platforms

Etsy and Upwork – If you're looking to start a small business with minimal investment, platforms like Etsy (for handmade goods or crafts) and Upwork (for freelancing and services) provide a great starting point. You can use these platforms to sell products, offer services, or build a portfolio, all from the comfort of your own home or student residence.

Shopify and Amazon – For students interested in e-commerce, platforms like Shopify and Amazon allow entrepreneurs to create online stores, manage inventory, and reach customers worldwide. These tools simplify the process of setting up a business and selling products.

Community Networks and Competitions

Student Entrepreneur Networks – Connecting with other student entrepreneurs can provide a great source of support. Look for student clubs or online networks that connect young entrepreneurs. These communities offer advice, share resources, and often work together on projects or events.

Business Plan Competitions – Many colleges, universities, and organizations host business plan competitions, offering cash prizes, mentorship, and access to investors. Competing in these events allows students to showcase their business ideas and get feedback from industry professionals.

Career Development and Job Search Resources

If you're looking for a job or internship while building entrepreneurial skills, check out these platforms:

SAYouth.mobi – A government-backed, zero-rated platform connecting unemployed youth with job listings, training programs, and internship opportunities.

JobJack – An entry-level job portal that helps young South Africans find part-time, full-time, and temporary employment opportunities.

LinkedIn – The world's largest professional networking platform, ideal for building a professional brand, connecting with industry experts, and applying for jobs.

Sangonet NGO Pulse – A job portal for opportunities in nonprofit organizations, education, and social impact fields, perfect for students interested in advocacy or social entrepreneurship.

University Career Fairs & Workshops – Many universities host career expos, networking events, and training workshops where students can meet employers, gain industry insights, and prepare for job applications.

Government Initiatives Addressing Youth Unemployment

Given South Africa's high youth unemployment rate (46.6% as of Q3, 2024), the government has implemented several employment and entrepreneurship programs to support young people.

Presidential Youth Employment Intervention (PYEI) – A coordinated effort by the South African government to address youth unemployment by connecting young people with learning, work experience, and business development opportunities.

- **The National Pathway Management Network** – A centralized job and training platform connecting youth with employment programs.

- **SAYouth.mobi** – A free, government-backed job search platform for young South Africans.

- **Demand-led Skilling Programs** – Focuses on closing the skills gap by offering training aligned with employer needs.

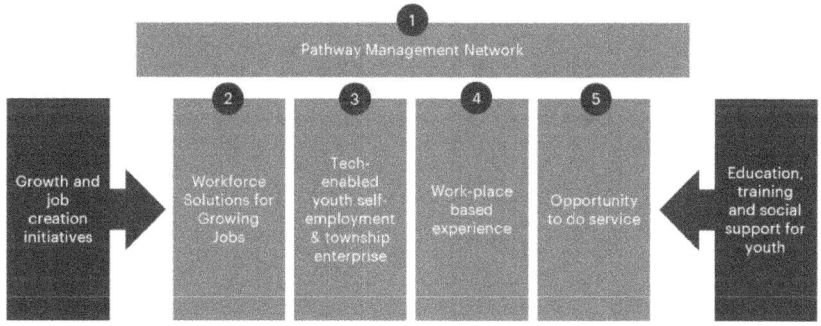

5by5 Plan – A government initiative launched in 2019 to create 2 million jobs for young people through:

- Strengthening job placement programs.

- Expanding work-based learning initiatives.

- Promoting small business development and self-employment opportunities.

- Increasing access to volunteering and internship programs.

Harambee Youth Employment Accelerator – Works with public and private sectors to bridge the gap between job seekers and employers. Provides free training, interview coaching, and job placement assistance.

National Youth Service (NYS) – Offers short-term work experience programs to help young people gain practical skills, build work readiness, and earn a stipend while training.

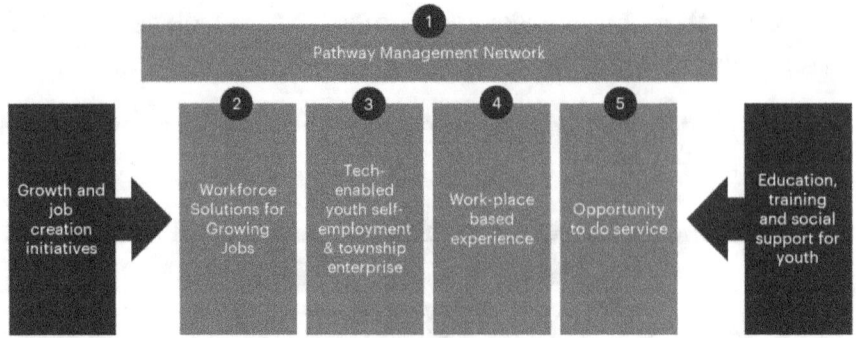

Offline Platforms and Events for Job Seekers

Not all career opportunities are found online. Many valuable connections happen at in-person events. Consider attending:

SAYouth National Opportunities Roadshow – A nationwide event where youth engage with employers, explore job openings, and attend skills development workshops.

Motsepe Foundation Information & Opportunities Expo – A career development event that connects young professionals with corporate, government, and nonprofit leaders.

Provincial Youth Career Expos – Government-led job fairs that provide students with career guidance, skills training, and networking opportunities.

University or College Career Fairs – A great way for students to meet recruiters, attend workshops, and explore potential career paths.

Career Workshops and Seminars: Enhancing Employability

To remain competitive in the job market, students should continuously develop their skills. Attending career workshops and professional development programs helps with the following:

Expanding Industry Knowledge – Learning about career paths, industry trends, and skill-building opportunities.

Developing New Skills – Workshops often offer training in resume writing, interview techniques, and personal branding.

Networking with Professionals – Building social capital by meeting recruiters, mentors, and professionals in various fields.

Recommended career development resources

LinkedIn Learning & Alison – Offers free and affordable courses on career development, business skills, and industry-specific training.

One Young World Summit – A global leadership event connecting young professionals with world leaders, entrepreneurs, and industry experts.

African Youth Summit – A pan-African career and entrepreneurship summit focused on youth-led solutions to tackle unemployment.

With youth unemployment at crisis levels, students must take advantage of career resources, employability programs, and entrepreneurial opportunities. Whether you're planning to launch a business, secure an internship, or explore government-backed job initiatives, the key is to stay proactive, build relevant skills, and take advantage of available opportunities.

Reflections and Takeaways

As we wrap up this chapter on the entrepreneurial mindset, it's important to reflect on the key lessons learned and think about how to take action moving forward.

Key Takeaways:

1. **Entrepreneurship is a Mindset:** At its core, entrepreneurship is about thinking differently. It's about spotting opportunities, solving problems, and taking initiative. Whether or not you decide to start a business, an entrepreneurial mindset will help you in every area of your life—from your studies to your career.

2. **Resilience, Creativity, and Persistence:** Building a business takes time, effort, and perseverance. You'll face challenges, but it's important to keep pushing forward, learn from your failures, and keep refining your approach. The most successful entrepreneurs are the ones who keep going, even when things get tough.

3. **Taking the initiative:** It all starts with taking the first step. Don't wait for the perfect moment—start with what you have, even if it's small. Every successful entrepreneur starts with an idea, a spark of curiosity, and the willingness to try.

Journal Prompt:

- Think about your entrepreneurial goals.

- What's one small step you can take right now to move closer to achieving them?

- It could be researching an idea or exploring potential opportunities.

- You could also join an entrepreneurial club or community for support.

- Consider sketching out your business plan or writing down your goals.

- Focus on taking immediate, actionable steps—no matter how small they seem.

- These small actions will add up over time and bring you closer to your dreams.

A World of Possibilities

As you finish reading this chapter, remember that the world of entrepreneurship is open to everyone. With the right mindset, anyone can become an entrepreneur. The key is to stay curious, embrace challenges, and always be ready to learn and grow.

Entrepreneurship Is Accessible to All:

No matter where you come from or what resources you have, entrepreneurship is within your reach. Your unique perspective, experiences, and ideas can all contribute to building something valuable.

Don't wait for the "perfect time" to start; that moment is now. Begin with small steps, keep your goals in sight, and take action. The world is full of possibilities, and your ideas have the potential to create meaningful change.

Motivational Quote:

"Dream big, start small, and act now—the world is waiting for your ideas."

– **Unknown**

Chapter 11:

A Mother's Prayer

A Letter to My Child

In the quiet of the night, as I write this letter to you, my heart is full of emotions I cannot adequately put into words.

My Dearest Child,

As you stand at the edge of a new chapter, about to step into the world on your own, I am filled with an overwhelming sense of pride. Watching you grow into the strong, independent person you are today has been the greatest joy of my life. But alongside that pride, there is a gentle ache in my heart. I worry about you—about the challenges you will face, the mistakes you might make, and the obstacles you will encounter. I hope that you remember that no matter where life takes you, I will always be here, cheering you on, praying for you, and loving you with all my heart.

This moment is bittersweet, isn't it? The world is vast, and you're stepping into it with wide-eyed wonder. I want you to know that no matter how far you go, my love will be your constant companion. I hope that in every moment of joy, and even in times of doubt, you'll remember that you have a family that believes in you unconditionally.

Remember, the world will not always be kind. It will challenge you, test your limits, and push you to places you never thought you could go. But in those moments, I want you to hold onto one truth: *you are never alone.* You carry with you the love and strength of everyone who has stood by you, and that is a force stronger than any difficulty you may face.

I trust that you will navigate this journey with courage, resilience, and grace. You are ready, my child, ready to take on whatever comes your way. Just as I have always been here for you, I know that you will find your own way to light up the world.

With all the love in my heart,
Mom

A Tale of Two Pandemics

As I sit here, reflecting on my journey as a Psychosocial Development Officer at Naledi Hospice in Bloemfontein, the City of Roses in the Free State Province of South Africa, I am struck by the cruel irony of fate. Twenty-four years ago, I witnessed the devastating impact of the HIV and AIDS pandemic on children, leaving them orphaned and vulnerable. Today, I find myself facing a different pandemic, one that threatens the very fabric of our society: gender-based violence and femicide (GBVF).

In the early 2000s, I worked with children and adults affected by HIV and AIDS. It was a time of great uncertainty and fear. The disease was ravaging communities, leaving countless children without parents or caregivers. I remember the tears, the sense of hopelessness, and the overwhelming burden that many young people had to carry. Child-headed households became a common phenomenon, where children—some as young as ten—took on adult responsibilities, caring for their siblings, managing the household, and struggling to access education and healthcare.

But amidst the grief, there was hope. With the introduction of ART (antiretroviral therapy) in the early 2000s, lives were transformed. I saw children regain their childhoods, families find healing, and communities rebuild themselves through compassion and resilience.

Fast-forward twenty years, and I now see a new crisis devastating our communities. GBVF has become a pandemic of its own, claiming the lives of countless women and children. Just as HIV/AIDS once tore families apart, today, it is violence and fear deeply affect our homes, universities, and workplaces. The tables have turned—where once children were orphaned, now mothers are burying their daughters, sisters, and loved ones.

This realization led me to ask myself: How can I ensure that no other mother has to endure such pain? How can we, as a society, prevent another young life from being cut short by senseless violence?

The Impact of Losing a Parent

Losing a parent is never easy, but losing one to HIV and AIDS was particularly difficult. The stigma and shame surrounding the disease made it hard for children to speak about their grief. Many were forced to drop out of school to become caregivers, while others were left vulnerable to exploitation and poverty. The grief was overwhelming, but so was the strength they found in each other.

As a Psychosocial Development Officer, I worked with these children, helping them process their emotions through counseling, play therapy, and memory box projects. A simple box—filled with letters, photos, and souvenirs—became a lifeline of love, a way for them to hold onto their parents' memory.

Today, as we face GBVF, I see mothers grieving their daughters, just as children once grieved their lost parents. The cycle of loss continues, but so does the fight for justice, healing, and change.

Creating a Safe Space

As a Psychosocial Development Officer, I have had the profound privilege of working with children who have endured loss and grief. My experience at a hospice has granted me a unique understanding of the emotional and psychological toll of death on families, especially children.

In my role, along with many others in the field, I was responsible for creating a safe and supportive environment where children felt comfortable expressing their emotions. I learned the importance of validating their feelings and acknowledging their pain rather than dismissing or minimizing it. We encouraged emotional expression through play therapy, art, and open discussions, providing them with a sense of control over their environment and emotions.

A child's grief is complex. Without proper support systems, it can manifest in anger, withdrawal, and anxiety. Our goal was to offer these children tools to navigate their pain, helping them find healing through connection, understanding, and self-expression.

The Gift of Compassion: Integrated Palliative Care for a Child's Grief

Palliative care, as defined by the World Health Organization (WHO), is an approach that improves the quality of life for patients and their families facing life-threatening illness. It provides relief from pain, addresses psychological distress, and offers holistic emotional and spiritual support.

I worked with a team from different areas led by a palliative care physician whose gentle bedside manner provided a beacon of hope to grieving families. Our team included professional nurses who offered compassionate medical care, a social worker who helped connect families to support services, and a spiritual care provider who provided emotional support and guidance.

Together, we took a comprehensive approach to care—understanding that physical, emotional, and spiritual well-being are all connected. Our team listened to stories, validated emotions, and provided personalized support to those struggling with grief, loss, and the uncertainties of terminal illness.

This experience not only shaped my professional journey but also my personal understanding of healing and resilience. The gift of palliative care is not just about managing illness—it's about preserving dignity, offering emotional support, and creating space for comfort, connection, and healing. As I reflect on this work, I realize that integrated palliative care was not only a service to others but a journey of healing for me as well.

A Misconception About Hospice Care

Too often, hospice care is misunderstood. Many believe that hospices are only for those in the final stages of life, a place where people go to wait for the end. But this could not be further from the truth.

Hospice care is not about death—it is about compassionate living. It is about ensuring that individuals facing life-limiting illnesses receive the holistic, dignified care they deserve.

Palliative care is not just about managing pain—it is about addressing the emotional, spiritual, and psychological needs of both patients and their families. It is about bringing comfort, providing guidance, and ensuring that no one faces their journey alone.

As I reflect on my experiences in hospice work, I see that true care extends beyond medicine. It is found in kindness, in presence, in creating moments of love and dignity.

It is time to reshape the narrative—to recognize that hospice care is not about waiting for life to end but about making every moment meaningful.

A Legacy of Compassion

The true measure of life is not just in what we leave behind but in the kindness we show while we are still here. Compassion is the foundation of healing—it is found in the hands that care for the sick, the voices that speak for the unheard, and the hearts that choose to love despite adversity.

Palliative care is more than medical treatment; it is a testament to humanity's ability to comfort, nurture, and uplift one another. In the moments of deepest grief, it is compassion that provides light. And in the face of loss, it is the love we give that defines the legacy we leave.

The Power of Unconditional Love

Unconditional love—the kind of love that a parent or guardian offers—is one of the most powerful forces in a young person's life. It's the quiet, steadfast belief in your potential, even when you doubt yourself. It's the foundation of your strength and what carries you through life's most difficult moments.

The Strength of Parental Love

Parents are the quiet warriors in your life. When you stumble, they are there to lift you. When you falter, they believe in you. Even when you face failure, your love remains constant. They never stop seeing the best in you, even when you struggle to see it in yourself.

Take Nia's story, for example. She was rejected from her dream university and devastated by the disappointment; she called her mother. The first words she heard were, "This is just a detour, my love. We'll find another way." Nia's mother's unwavering belief in her, even when the world seemed to say otherwise, gave her the strength to keep trying. With time, Nia found her place at a university she hadn't even considered—and flourished.

This kind of love is not only about comforting words—it's about the deep-rooted belief that, no matter what, your child is capable of greatness. That belief doesn't falter when times get tough; it only grows stronger, urging you to keep going and to rise from every setback.

How You Can Honor This Love:

As learners and students, it's easy to get lost in your own struggles and forget the sacrifices others make for you. But remember that the love of your parents or guardians is a gift—a guidepost that helps you navigate life's uncertainties. You honor this love by showing gratitude, by persevering even when things get hard, and by giving back in your own way.

Quote:

"A parent's love is a guidepost through life's uncertainties."

Honor the love that has been given to you by honoring your own journey. Every step you take towards success is a tribute to the sacrifices and strength that your parents have invested in you.

The Rise of a New Pandemic

Just as HIV/AIDS once robbed us of an entire generation, GBVF threatens the lives and futures of our daughters, mothers, and sisters. We cannot ignore the reality that:

A future was envisioned but never realized.

A young girl dreamed of becoming a doctor, but her life was stolen from her.

A mother worked tirelessly for a better life, only to have hers taken away.

But we can create a different future. A future where our daughters grow up safe, where our sons learn respect, where love triumphs over fear. It starts with us.

A Future Reimagined:

- Creating safe spaces for survivors and their families.

- Educating young people about healthy relationships and consent.

- Holding institutions accountable for addressing violence and discrimination.

- Supporting community-based organizations that provide counseling, shelter, and legal assistance.

Our history has shown us the cost of inaction. If we fail to address GBVF with the same urgency that we tackled the HIV/AIDS crisis, we risk allowing yet another generation to be lost. The time for awareness has passed; now is the time for real intervention, policies that protect, and a commitment to ensuring that no more lives are taken before their time.

The Irony of Time

As I reflect on my journey, I am struck by the cruel irony of time. Reflecting on the past, I see how one crisis gives way to another. Where once we lost parents to illness, today, we lose daughters to violence. It is a painful reminder that while history may change its course, the grief of loss remains unchanged. Our duty now is not just to remember but to fight for a world where cycles of suffering do not repeat.

Then, we were fighting a pandemic that stole parents from their children; now, we face another crisis that robs children of their mothers. The grief is just as deep, the wounds just as raw. It forces us to ask: How many more futures must be lost before we create lasting change?

The Loss of a Future Envisaged

Each life lost to GBVF is not just a tragedy—it is the loss of a future that was meant to be written.

I think of the young girls who once dreamed of becoming doctors, lawyers, or pilots—whose journeys were cut short by senseless violence. I think of the young boys who aspired to be scientists, artists, or engineers—but whose futures were stolen from them. I think of the mothers who worked tirelessly to create better lives for their children—only to have their own lives taken before they could see their dreams fulfilled.

Every life lost represents a promise left unfulfilled—a light extinguished before it could shine at its brightest. These individuals were not just statistics; they were someone's child, someone's sibling, someone's friend. They had hopes, ambitions, and the potential to change the world.

A Future Reimagined

Let us recommit ourselves to creating a world where every:

- Child grows up with hope and promise.

- Women can live freely and without fear.

- Individual has the chance to fulfill their potential.

The future is not predetermined—it is something we shape through our choices, our actions, and our commitment to change. Together, we can turn pain into progress. Together, we can make a difference.

Resilience and Perseverance

Many children, especially those in child-headed households, were forced to grow up too quickly. They faced immense hardships—caring for siblings, navigating grief, and fighting against a world that seemed indifferent to their struggles.

Yet, despite these challenges, they learned invaluable lessons about resilience and perseverance. They discovered that even in the darkest moments, hope can exist.

Grief is not linear. There are days when it feels overwhelming when the weight of loss threatens to consume every part of you. But the most important thing is to let yourself feel, to acknowledge the pain, and to move at your own pace. Healing is not about forgetting—it is about learning to carry love and loss together, side by side.

For many, education became the key to breaking the cycle of poverty and creating a better future. It was the one thing they could hold onto—their chance at a new beginning, their way to reclaim the future that had once seemed lost.

A Memory Box of Love

Throughout my career, I have witnessed individuals facing terminal illness make extraordinary efforts to leave behind something meaningful for their loved ones.

Even as their hands grew weak and their bodies frail, their spirit remained strong. They wrote letters, recorded messages, and prepared memory boxes—a collection of letters, photographs, and mementos that would serve as a tangible connection to their memory.

I have seen children open these boxes, tears streaming down their faces as they read the words of their parents, holding onto the fragments of love and wisdom left behind.

Today, technology allows us even greater ways of preserving memories, but the essence remains the same. A memory box is not just a collection of objects—it is a testament to love, resilience, and the desire to be present even in absence.

Reflection on Growth and Transformation

As parents watch their children take their first steps toward independence, they often experience a complex mix of emotions. Pride, joy, worry, and sometimes even a tinge of sadness as they realize how much their child has grown. This transition—from child to young adult—is both a milestone and a process of continuous transformation, not just for the student but for the parents as well.

Emotional Elements

Trauma and Shock – The sudden loss of a parent can be deeply traumatic, especially when combined with the stigma and shame surrounding HIV and AIDS.

Guilt and Self-Blame – Many children feel guilty for not being able to do more, for not preventing the loss of their parent, or for not being strong enough to carry their family's burdens.

Anger and Frustration – The weight of loss can lead to anger, especially when it is paired with the responsibility of caring for younger siblings.

Sadness and Depression – Prolonged grief, isolation, and lack of support can make healing seem impossible.

The Importance of Community-Based Organizations

To truly support those affected by HIV, AIDS, and GBVF, we must recognize the role of community-based care:

Home-Based Care & Support Groups – Providing emotional and practical support for children and families.

Faith-Based Organizations – Offering spiritual counseling, healing, and a sense of belonging.

NGOs & Community-Based Organizations (CBOs) – Providing education, counseling, economic support, and advocacy.

Holistic Palliative Care – Addressing the physical, emotional, and spiritual needs of families facing loss.

A Parent's Prayer for the Future

As this chapter draws to a close, it's time to leave readers with a prayer—a prayer that encapsulates all the hopes and wishes that parents have for their children. It's a moment of connection, of asking for guidance and protection, and of reaffirming the belief that, with faith, anything is possible.

A Heartfelt Prayer:

"Dear Lord,

We come before you today with grateful hearts, asking for Your protection over our children as they step into the future. We pray that You grant them wisdom, strength, and resilience to face the challenges ahead. May they find their purpose and walk in it with confidence, knowing that they are not alone. Bless them with good health, success, and happiness. And above all, may they always remember that they are loved—unconditionally and forever.

Guide them through their journey of growth and independence, and help us, as parents, to trust in their ability to navigate life's obstacles. We know that with Your guidance and our love, they can overcome anything that comes their way. We place their future in Your hands, trusting that You will guide them to the path meant for them.

Amen.

Motivational Quote:

"Faith is the bridge between where you are and where you want to be."

This quote speaks to the importance of belief—not just in the process of growth and change, but in the strength that comes from faith. It serves as a reminder that faith and belief in oneself can help overcome any challenge, turning obstacles into stepping stones toward success.

Chapter 12:

Faith in the Education System

Khumalo attended the University Church Service for the first time on Sunday with his friend Tshepo who is doing the pursuing degree program. He comes from a family where religion was rarely, if ever, discussed, so this was a completely new experience for him. However, the friend of his friend who brought him along were very kind and welcoming toward Khumalo.

He was surprised at the dancing and jovial atmosphere among his peers, how they interacted with each other especially given that it was a Sunday morning at the university chapel. After the service, Khumalo was introduced to the Pastor Though many questions filled his mind, he was too shy to ask them. It was then arranged that the Pastor will meet with Khumalo on Thursday before the weekly Student bible study held on campus.

Khumalo was very excited as the pastor had encouraged him to write down all his questions so they could discuss them on Thursday. That Sunday evening, Khumalo lay on his bed, staring at the ceiling and reflecting on everything that had happened earlier that day. He wondered how his fellow students could be so happy and joyful, while he, Khumalo, had so many unanswered questions. He wondered, "Don't they have questions too?"

why his parents or older siblings had never shared anything with him about the Bible, God, or religion. He then remembered his grandmother, who used to sing choruses in the kitchen and always prayed for her grandchildren. His parents, however, never followed her example.

Khumalo then asked himself, Is there a God? Who is God? Where is God? How can a person say there is a God when you cannot see Him? He further remembered the funeral of his grandma, where the pastor also spoke about God and the good deeds she had done in the community. Khumalo then said to himself that he would speak to Tshepo the next day about this "God issue" and hear what he had to say.

During lunchtime the next day on campus, Khumalo met with Tshepo and asked him about the church service. Why did Tshepo invite him? What purpose did Tshepo find in attending church services? It was at this point that Tshepo shared his testimony with Khumalo, how he had survived a near-fatal car accident during his matric year, and how, while lying there bleeding in the wreckage, he had promised God that if he were spared, he would give his heart to Jesus and accept Him as his Saviour.

At this point, Khumalo became very intrigued and asked Tshepo, Do you mean you spoke to God? How do you know He listens to you? Tshepo replied that he believes he is alive today because God spared his life, and so, after the accident, he joined a local church to honour the promise he had made while lying there, half-alive and half-dead.

The conversation stayed with Khumalo that night. It left him with even more questions about God and religion. Slowly, he began to make sense of the sermon the pastor had preached last Sunday. He was now preparing himself for the Thursday meeting with the pastor, especially after all the spiritual encounters he had experienced and listened to for the first time in his life.

That Thursday morning, Khumalo got up and went to his classes, but the ever-repeating thoughts about what would happen that evening during his meeting with the Pastor kept coming back to him. Throughout the day in the lab, he found himself constantly thinking about the meeting. At one point, he was so deep in thought that he didn't even realize the professor had asked him a question during the session.

It was at that moment that Khumalo asked the professor whether he believed there was a God, especially in the context of the science experiment they were working on. The professor was visibly surprised by the question but responded that, yes, some people do believe in God, while others believe in evolution. He then added that he personally believed in the latter.

After the lab session, the professor asked Khumalo to meet with him. During that meeting that afternoon, Khumalo shared that he would be meeting with the Pastor or University Chaplain that same evening to learn more about the God that others say they believe in.

That evening, just before the weekly Student Youth Bible Study on campus, Khumalo met with the Pastor. He was surprised by how openly the Pastor allowed him to ask questions and express himself freely. The Pastor simply listened, without interjecting or interrupting.

In particular, Khumalo remembered the Bible verse the Pastor had quoted the previous Sunday, John 3:16: "For God so loved the world that He gave His only begotten Son, that whoever believes in Him should not perish but have everlasting life." Khumalo then asked, How can a God you cannot see promise a person everlasting life? Where is the evidence that everlasting life exists? Is this just a hoax or is it real?

Instead of answering directly, the Pastor asked if he could share his own personal life story. Khumalo agreed.

The Pastor then shared that he grew up in a very rural, dusty part of South Africa, with no streetlights, no tarred roads, and having to use outdoor pit latrine toilets. There was no hot or cold running water in the home. They had to fetch water from the river, and any hot water had to be boiled over a fire made from wood.

At this point, Khumalo became so intrigued by the Pastor's story that he didn't even notice some of his university friends passing by in the corridor. The Pastor continued, explaining that he never knew who his father was. He was raised by his grandmother because his mother worked in the city and only returned home on weekends to provide for the family.

Khumalo then interjected and asked, "Why did you become a priest?"

The Pastor paused, looked up at the sky, and replied that he had always wanted to be of service to his fellow citizens. He wanted to give back to the community he came from. He then shared that he had a near-death experience when he was knocked down by a car, an accident that left him with a physical walking disability. After the accident, the Pastor said he made a promise to God: that if he survived, he would dedicate his life to God's work. It was that promise, he explained, that led him to go to seminary and become a priest.

Khumalo was deeply moved by the story. After checking the time on his watch, both he and the Pastor realised it was time for the weekly student Bible study session, which they then attended together. The session went well but it once again stirred many questions in Khumalo's mind.

That evening, back at his residence, Khumalo reflected deeply on his conversation with the Pastor. Though still confused about this whole "God issue," he told himself not to overthink it and decided to focus on his academic work instead. Yet, questions lingered. Why would God allow him to grow up without a father? Why did his mother have to work so hard just to provide for them?

He began to reflect on his own life, his circumstances, his emotions, and the unanswered questions he carried. In the midst of this introspection, his phone rang. It was Lwethu, a student he had befriended during his first few days at university. She was clearly in distress, she had just been robbed outside the off-campus canteen and needed help.

Though it was late at night, Khumalo didn't hesitate. Still in his day clothes, he rushed out of his residence and ran toward the university gate. When he arrived, Lwethu was visibly shaken. He gently embraced her and assured her that everything would be okay. Thankfully, she was not physically harmed, just left traumatized by the experience.

After the police had taken her statement, the two of them walked back through the campus gates toward the student residence. During the walk, Lwethu turned to Khumalo and asked a surprising question in a trembling voice: "Do you believe in God? Or in some Higher Being... some Eternal Force?"

Khumalo stopped in his tracks. "Why would you ask me that?" he replied.

Lwethu answered, "Because you're so compassionate. You have this calm, loving spirit that most people don't have. I called four other students tonight, but they were all too busy. You came immediately. I don't even know what you were doing, but you dropped everything for me. It feels like... like there's a part of God in you. Like you were sent."

She paused, then added, "I don't go to church much here. But I do believe in God and tonight, I believe He sent me an angel. That angel was you."

Khumalo was stunned. "Err... err... I'm not even sure what I believe about God," he stammered. "I still have serious questions."

By then, they had reached the residence. She quietly returned to her room, and Khumalo to his.

Alone in his room, something shifted. A strange peace washed over him. Without knowing why, tears rolled down his cheeks and he began to weep uncontrollably. Then, for the first time in his life, Khumalo knelt beside his bed and prayed. He asked God to come into his heart. That night, he accepted the Lord Jesus as his personal Saviour.

He still had questions. But what he felt in that moment couldn't be explained. An inner peace, deeper than understanding, settled over him. He couldn't contain the joy and relief he felt.

The next day, Khumalo went straight to the Campus Chaplain's office and shared what had happened. The Chaplain embraced him with both arms and said, "This is just the beginning of your journey. There will be challenges, but if you stay focused, keep your faith, and work hard in your studies, you'll see the success you were made for."

Reflection prompt:

- Are there aspects of Khumalo's life that you can personally relate to? If so, what are they?
- Do you also have doubts about the existence of God? Where do you turn with those questions?
- What elements of Khumalo's upbringing resonate with your own? How have you processed or navigated those experiences?

Campus experience:

- What is your personal view on God? Do you believe such a being exists?
- How do you feel about the way Khumalo dealt with the questions on his heart? Would you have approached it differently?
- What was the last major crisis you faced at school or university? Did someone come to your aid during that time?

- What are your thoughts on Khumalo having such a deep and personal experience with God? Does it make you feel distant or disconnected or does it encourage you to reflect more deeply on your own life? Write your thoughts in your journal or diary.

Motivational Quote:

"Doubt stifles and kills initiatives, but Faith opens the door that leads to many other doors of wonderful lifelong experiences."

Chapter 13:

Turning Points and New Beginnings

The Semester That Changed Everything

Mbali's story is one of transformation—a narrative that speaks to the heart of personal growth. A few semesters ago, she was struggling with failing grades, feeling disconnected from her studies, and unsure about her future. Her confidence was at an all-time low, and she began questioning her place in university. But everything changed after one pivotal moment: a conversation with her mentor, who encouraged her to reflect on her strengths and passions and to reframe her challenges as opportunities for growth.

At first, Mbali was resistant. How could she possibly turn things around? But as she reflected on her journey, she realized that this moment of struggle could be the turning point she needed. From that moment forward, she took ownership of her journey. She implemented better time management, sought help when needed, and prioritized self-care. Over the course of that semester, Mbali's grades improved, but more importantly, her perspective on herself and her potential shifted.

Key Takeaways:

- **Personal Triumph Through Determination:** Mbali's academic struggles were not the end of her story but the beginning. With self-reflection, determination, and the willingness to seek help, she turned her failures into the foundation of future success.

- **Self-Reflection and Action**: It was her ability to reflect on her struggles and take actionable steps toward change that made all the difference.

As you read Mbali's story, think about your own academic journey. Have there been moments of struggle that, with the right mindset, could become stepping stones to success? Reflecting on these turning points is the first step toward embracing change in a meaningful way.

Embracing Change and Uncertainty

Change is an inevitable part of life, especially during your transition to higher education. But how you respond to change can make all the difference. Many students fear change because it often comes with uncertainty. What will the next semester be like? Will you be able to handle the pressure of exams and assignments? These questions are common, but they also offer an opportunity for growth. Embracing change means stepping into the unknown with the belief that you can navigate whatever challenges arise.

Understanding Change:

Change, by its nature, is uncomfortable. It disrupts the status quo and forces us to confront new realities. Whether it's a shift in your academic performance, a change in your social circle, or adjusting to new responsibilities, uncertainty can feel overwhelming. However, it's important to recognize that growth happens when we are stretched beyond our comfort zones.

Practical Strategies for Navigating Change:

- **Mindfulness**: Practice staying present and grounded in the face of uncertainty. By focusing on the here and now, you can reduce anxiety and increase your ability to handle change with clarity.

- **Goal-Setting**: Break down your larger goals into smaller, manageable tasks. Setting clear, achievable goals can help you navigate uncertainty and stay focused on what you can control.

- **Seeking Guidance:** Don't hesitate to seek support from mentors, counselors, or peers. Sometimes, a fresh perspective or a word of encouragement can provide the confidence you need to move forward.

Reflection Prompt:

- Think about a time when you experienced a significant change in your life.

- How did you grow through that experience?

- What lessons did you learn about yourself during this time?

- Reflect on how facing this change made you more resilient.

- How can you apply these lessons to future challenges or changes?

Recognizing Turning Points

A turning point in life is a moment that marks a clear shift in perspective, behavior, or direction. It's the point at which you look back and realize that something has fundamentally changed. Turning points are not always easy to recognize at the moment, but when you do, you begin to see them as opportunities for profound growth.

What Is a Turning Point?

A turning point is often defined by moments of clarity or action—those times when you decide to change your direction, redefine your goals, or take decisive action toward the life you want. These moments can be big—like overcoming a failure, finding a career path, or achieving a major academic goal—or they can be small, like deciding to prioritize your mental health, learning a new skill, or changing your daily routine.

Examples of Turning Points:

- **Overcoming Failure:** Many students experience a turning point after failing an exam or course. Instead of seeing failure as an end, they learn to view it as an opportunity to reevaluate their approach, study habits, or mindset. For example, after a disappointing first semester, Sipho made the decision to get serious about time management and seek academic support. This decision ultimately turned his academic career around.

- **Finding Passion:** Another example could be discovering a passion for a subject or career path. Maybe you started university uncertain about your major but later found a deep interest in a particular field. This newfound passion can shift your entire academic and career trajectory.

Exercise: Write About a Personal Turning Point

"Think about a turning point in your life—big or small. How did this moment change you? How did it shape your current path?"

This exercise asks readers to reflect on their own turning points, helping them recognize moments that have shaped their journey and consider how they've grown as a result.

Reinventing Yourself

In life, we are all bound to face moments that shake us to our core—times when everything seems to crumble around us. But it is in those moments that we are given the chance to reinvent ourselves, to emerge from adversity stronger, wiser, and more capable than before. Reinvention doesn't mean abandoning who you are; it means evolving and growing into the person you were always meant to be.

Embracing a Growth Mindset:

A key part of reinvention is adopting a growth mindset. This mindset revolves around the idea that our abilities and intelligence are not fixed but can be developed over time through dedication, effort, and learning. When you face a setback or failure, you don't see it as a permanent defeat. Instead, you see it as an opportunity to learn, adapt, and improve.

Think back to a time when you didn't succeed at something—whether it was a test, a relationship, or a personal goal. How did you handle it? Did you let the failure define you, or did you use it as a stepping stone to something greater?

Steps to Self-Reinvention:

1. **Identify Your Strengths**: The first step in reinventing yourself is recognizing your inherent strengths. What do you excel at? What do you enjoy doing? Identifying these strengths will help you figure out where to direct your energy as you evolve. Take time to reflect on your talents, skills, and passions.

2. **Set Clear Goals**: Reinvention requires purpose. Setting both short-term and long-term goals will give you a sense of direction. Break your larger goals into smaller, manageable steps. This will allow you to measure progress and feel motivated along the way.

3. **Take Consistent Action**: Reinvention doesn't happen overnight. It requires consistent effort, even when the road gets tough. Start with small, manageable changes in your daily routine. Each action, no matter how small, moves you closer to your desired future.

Motivational Quote:

"You are never too old to set another goal or to dream a new dream."

– C.S. Lewis.

This quote is a reminder that reinvention is always possible, no matter where you are in life. You have the power to shape your future.

The Role of Support Systems

No one achieves greatness alone. As we journey through life, the importance of having a strong support system cannot be overstated. Support systems are made up of mentors, friends, family, and peers—each playing a unique role in guiding us through challenges. These people lift us up, offer advice when needed, and remind us of our strengths when we doubt ourselves.

How Mentors, Friends, and Family Provide Guidance:

- **Mentors:** Mentors offer guidance based on experience. They help us navigate through life's challenges by sharing their own lessons learned. A mentor doesn't simply tell you what to do—they guide you in discovering your own path and solutions.

- **Friends:** Friends are the emotional anchors that keep us grounded. In moments of doubt or hardship, friends offer a listening ear and provide comfort. They remind us that we are not alone, even when life feels overwhelming.

- **Family:** Family serves as our most foundational support. Whether it's a parent, sibling, or guardian, their unwavering belief in us often provides the courage to move forward, even when the journey gets tough.

Building a Supportive Network:

Support systems aren't just something we lean on in times of crisis—they are essential for our daily growth. Building a strong network involves surrounding yourself with people who challenge you, encourage you, and support your dreams. These relationships should be reciprocal—where both parties give and receive support.

Gratitude Exercise:

"Think of three people who have had a positive influence on your growth. What has each person contributed to your life, and how can you show them gratitude today?"

This exercise encourages readers to reflect on their support systems and deepen their appreciation for the people who help them succeed.

Lessons Learned from Adversity

Life's most difficult moments often become our greatest teachers. Adversity, while uncomfortable, pushes us to grow and become more resilient. It's through hardship that we develop patience, self-awareness, and the skills to overcome future challenges. The key to dealing with adversity is recognizing the lessons it has to offer.

Adversity as a Teacher:

Adversity isn't a roadblock—it's a lesson in disguise. Think about the last difficult experience you faced. Perhaps it was failing an exam or dealing with a personal setback. In hindsight, what did that experience teach you? Did you learn to manage stress better? Did you discover your inner strength? These moments of hardship are an opportunity to develop resilience.

The ability to see adversity as an opportunity for growth is one of the greatest skills you can develop. Instead of asking, "Why me?" start asking, "What can I learn from this?" The lessons learned during difficult times will serve as a foundation for future success.

Self-Compassion and Acceptance:

In times of difficulty, it's essential to practice self-compassion. We often hold ourselves to impossibly high standards, especially in moments of failure. But adversity is a part of life, and it's okay to stumble. The key is not to be harsh on yourself but to accept that you are doing your best and that it's okay to fall short sometimes.

Reflection Prompt:

- Think of a time when you faced a challenge.

- What did that experience teach you about yourself?

- How did overcoming this challenge shape your current perspective on life?

- Reflect on the skills or strengths you developed during that time.

- How can you use this experience to handle future challenges?

Preparing for New Beginnings

Every new beginning comes with its own unique set of challenges and opportunities. Whether you're transitioning from high school to university, switching careers, or embarking on a personal project, starting a new phase of life requires intentional preparation. The key to navigating these transitions successfully lies in planning, setting realistic goals, and cultivating a mindset of optimism and resilience.

Setting Intentions and Realistic Goals:

The first step in preparing for any new beginning is to clarify your intentions. What do you want to achieve in this new chapter? Intentions are not just vague desires; they are clear, focused statements about what you hope to accomplish. Once your intentions are set, break them down into specific, realistic goals. Think about where you want to be in one year, five years, or even ten years.

Start by identifying the small steps that will lead you to those bigger goals. These small actions might involve learning new skills, connecting with new people, or organizing your time in a more efficient way.

Overcoming Fear of the Unknown:

It's natural to feel apprehensive about stepping into the unknown, especially when faced with change. The fear of failure, uncertainty, or the pressure to succeed can sometimes feel overwhelming. However, fear is a normal part of growth. You can manage it through planning and positive affirmations.

Planning gives you a clear sense of direction, reducing the fear that comes with not knowing what lies ahead. Break down your new venture into manageable tasks. This will not only reduce anxiety but also give you measurable milestones to track your progress.

Affirmations are another powerful tool to overcome fear. When you affirm your ability to succeed, you reinforce a positive mindset that propels you forward. Here are some examples of affirmations to use:

"I am capable of handling whatever comes my way."

"Each step I take brings me closer to my goal."

"I trust myself and my abilities to thrive in new situations."

Celebrating Small Victories:

While the end goal is important, it's the journey that counts. Celebrating small victories along the way keeps you motivated and reinforces the habit of recognizing progress. These small wins add up and keep your momentum going, no matter how big or small they may seem.

Take time to acknowledge your achievements. Whether it's completing a project, learning a new skill, or simply taking a step toward your goal, these moments are worth celebrating. Doing so will remind you of how far you've come and inspire you to keep going.

Reflections and Takeaways

As we close this chapter on turning points and new beginnings, it's important to reflect on the lessons learned. Life is filled with turning points—those pivotal moments that push us to grow, evolve, and take action. These moments are not always easy, but they are always transformative.

Life as a Series of Turning Points to Embrace:

Each chapter in life is a turning point, and each turning point offers a new opportunity for growth. Embrace the changes that come your way, whether they are planned or unexpected. They are stepping stones that guide you toward the next phase of your journey. Each new beginning brings the chance to rewrite your story, create new experiences, and become the person you are meant to be.

Recognizing and Celebrating Resilience:

Along the way, you will face setbacks, but resilience will determine your success. Resilience isn't about avoiding difficulty; it's about bouncing back after setbacks and continuing to push forward with determination. Life's challenges are the crucibles that test your resilience. Celebrate those moments when you overcame obstacles and kept going.

As you move forward, remember that every turning point is not just about the destination but about who you become in the process.

Journal Prompt:

"What's one thing you're excited to begin, and how will you approach it?"

This journal prompt encourages readers to reflect on the new beginnings they are experiencing, helping them clarify their approach and mindset as they embark on their next phase.

Closing: The Journey Continues

The journey of life is continuous. Every ending marks the start of something new, and each new chapter offers an opportunity for fresh beginnings, whether it's a new academic year, a new career path, or a personal transformation. No matter what stage you're at, always remember that growth is a constant process.

Emphasizing That Every Ending is a New Beginning:

Each chapter you close makes space for the next one to begin. Embrace endings as natural parts of life, for they lead you to new opportunities. Even when something you care about comes to an end, know that it is clearing the way for something new to enter your life. Every closing door opens another, often leading to even greater opportunities.

Motivational Quote:

"Every great journey begins with a single step."

– Lao Tzu.

This timeless quote serves as a reminder that big achievements start with small actions. No matter where you are in your journey, the first step is the most important one.

Chapter 14:

Nothing for us without us

A Circle of Stories

In a quiet room, the air filled with a sense of camaraderie, a group of students, parents, and educators gathered together. The table was set with refreshments, but the real feast lay in the stories shared by each person present. As they took turns telling their experiences—some joyful, others marked by struggle—what became clear was the unifying thread of resilience that connected them all.

Each person had faced challenges, whether academic, emotional, or personal, but they had also emerged stronger, wiser, and more determined. Parents spoke of their fears and hopes for their children's futures, students shared their triumphs over adversity, and educators reflected on the transformative power of education. The stories were diverse, but the themes were the same: the power of resilience, the importance of support, and the unspoken strength that comes from within when facing life's challenges.

This moment, where voices from different walks of life came together, emphasized the importance of shared experiences in fostering understanding, growth, and connection. As these stories were shared, it became clear that while every journey is unique, the path to success is often paved with struggle, perseverance, and, most importantly, the willingness to keep moving forward.

From this circle of stories, the voices of those who have faced challenges and emerged stronger set the stage for the testimonials and reflections that follow. These experiences remind us all that no matter where we come from or what obstacles we face, we can always find the strength to rise.

Testimonials from Students

The voices of students speak volumes, offering a rich tapestry of experiences that show not only the difficulty of academic and personal journeys but also the profound strength that each student possesses. In their own words, we hear stories of overcoming adversity, finding purpose, and growing through challenges. Their experiences serve as both inspiration and a reminder that the journey is not always easy, but it is always worth it.

Quotes and Anecdotes from Survey Participants:

"I remember the moment I almost gave up. My grades were slipping, and I felt like I had no support. But one conversation with my mom changed everything. She reminded me that I had already overcome so much and I could keep going. I did. And now, I'm proud to say I graduated with honors." – Zanele, Student.

"The hardest part for me was believing in myself. It wasn't the exams that scared me, but the fear of failure. My teacher pulled me aside and said, 'You are capable. Don't let fear define your future.' That gave me the courage to push forward, and I'm now pursuing my dream career in engineering." – Thabo, Student

These stories reflect the resilience that students develop when faced with academic pressure, personal challenges, or moments of doubt. But what stands out in every story is the ability to rise again, often with a renewed sense of purpose and drive. The role of mentors, family members, and personal reflection is evident in their paths to success.

Reflection Prompt:

- Think about the personal stories shared in this book.

- Which story resonated with you the most, and why?

- How did the resilience demonstrated in that story connect with your own experiences?

- Reflect on how this story has impacted your perspective on facing challenges.

Insights from Parents and Educators

While the stories of students are central to this journey, the voices of parents and educators play a crucial role in shaping the experiences of young learners. Their perspectives offer a deeper understanding of the challenges and triumphs students face, as well as the importance of guidance and support in the process of growth.

Testimonials about the Transformative Power of Education:

"I've always believed in my child's potential, but it wasn't until I saw her face adversity that I truly understood the power of education. It's not just about learning facts; it's about learning resilience, perseverance, and self-belief. When she faced a difficult class, I knew it was not just an academic challenge—it was a life lesson that would shape her future." – Mrs. Mthembu, Parent.

"I've been teaching for over 20 years, and what I've learned is that it's not always the smartest students who succeed—it's those who refuse to give up. I've seen students face tremendous struggles, yet it's their resilience that has made them stand out. I always tell my students: 'Failure is not the opposite of success; it's part of the process.'" – Mr. Khumalo, Educator.

These insights from parents and educators emphasize the transformative power of education, not just as a means to gain knowledge but as a catalyst for personal growth and resilience.

Education is not just about passing exams; it's about learning how to overcome obstacles, navigate life's challenges, and transform setbacks into stepping stones.

Advice for Students:

"You will face challenges, but remember that each one is an opportunity to grow. Be patient with yourself, trust the process, and lean on those around you for support. Education is a journey, not a race." – Mrs. Makgoba, Educator.

This advice highlights the importance of patience, determination, and community support as students navigate the ups and downs of their academic and personal lives. The key message here is that success is not just about achieving academic excellence; it's about growing through the journey.

Enhancement Tip:

Include an inspiring quote from an educator: "Education is the most powerful weapon which you can use to change the world." – Nelson Mandela.

This quote reinforces the idea that education is not just a personal achievement but a tool for broader change and transformation.

Key Takeaways from the Survey

The survey conducted throughout the course of this book reveals powerful insights into the shared experiences of students, parents, and educators. These findings not only validate many of the themes explored earlier but also shed light on the common threads that bind us in our journeys of growth and transformation.

Trends: Mentorship Benefits, Common Challenges, and Effective Strategies

From the survey results, one of the most prominent trends that emerged was the profound impact of mentorship. Students who had access to mentors reported higher levels of confidence and motivation, emphasizing the importance of having someone to turn to for advice, encouragement, and guidance. Many respondents highlighted that mentorship helped them navigate the challenges of school, personal growth, and future planning.

Another common theme was the challenge of balancing academic pressures with personal lives. Students reported stress from managing coursework, social expectations, and personal issues. However, those who sought support and were proactive in managing their time found better outcomes, particularly in areas of mental health and academic performance.

Effective strategies for overcoming obstacles included setting clear goals, practicing mindfulness, and maintaining a strong support network. The survey also found that students who engaged in regular reflection, whether through journaling or discussions with others, were more likely to overcome setbacks with resilience and clarity.

Data Visualization: Charts and Infographics for Clarity

To make these findings more accessible, here is a breakdown of key survey results:

- **Mentorship Impact:**

Percentage of students who felt supported by a mentor: 87%

Increase in confidence levels among mentored students: 43%

- **Challenges Faced by Students:**

Top three challenges reported by students:

1. Time Management (58%)

2. Academic Stress (47%)

3. Mental Health Struggles (41%)

- **Effective Strategies for Success:**

Most common strategies adopted by successful students:

1. Goal Setting (72%)

2. Seeking Support (65%)

3. Mindfulness & Stress Management (59%)

Interactive Element:

"Reflect on How These Insights Align with Your Own Experiences"

As you read through these key findings, take a moment to reflect on your own experiences. How do these insights resonate with your personal journey? Are there strategies you've used that helped you overcome challenges? Have you benefited from mentorship or found solace in a strong support network? Consider how you can apply what you have learned to your future challenges, both academically and personally.

Reflections on Growth and Connection

The journey of growth is never a solitary one. Throughout the chapters, we have explored how students, parents, and educators have navigated the complexities of education, personal development, and the challenges that come with it. But more than just overcoming difficulties, the true essence of growth lies in connection—how we connect with others, share our struggles, and build a community of support.

Acknowledge the Transformation of Students and Their Communities

The transformation of students throughout this journey has been nothing short of inspiring. Many students began with doubts about their abilities, but as they moved forward, they not only improved academically but also grew in confidence and resilience. Their personal growth is a testament to their perseverance, the guidance of mentors, and the support of their families and communities.

In parallel, the broader communities—families, educators, and even peer groups—also underwent transformations. Parents, initially unsure of how to support their children in the face of adversity, found new ways to engage, encourage, and provide a foundation of love and understanding. Educators, too, reflected on their own teaching practices, evolving to better support their students' emotional and intellectual needs.

Emphasize the Role of Connection in Fostering Resilience

At the heart of all growth and transformation is connection. Connection to others provides the support, understanding, and motivation necessary to navigate life's challenges. Whether through family bonds, friendships, mentorship, or the guidance of educators, it is these connections that help us rise stronger, no matter the obstacles.

Through the stories and reflections shared in this book, we see the power of community. When individuals come together, offering support, encouragement, and empathy, they create an environment where resilience can thrive. The journey is never easy, but with the right connections, it becomes possible to face challenges with renewed strength.

Journal Prompt:

- Reflect on your journey through this book.

- What lessons have stood out to you the most?

- Which pieces of advice or insights do you plan to carry forward as you face future challenges?

- Take a moment to journal about your key takeaway—whether it's the importance of resilience, the value of support systems, or the transformative power of education.

- Let this lesson guide your next steps as you continue to grow and navigate new challenges.

Gratitude and Acknowledgments

As we come to the close of this book, it is essential to pause and reflect on the gratitude we owe to those who have supported us along our journeys. It is easy to forget the quiet acts of love, encouragement, and wisdom that have shaped our growth. Whether from family members, teachers, mentors, or friends, these people have been integral in helping us overcome obstacles and reach new heights.

Thank Contributors, Readers, and Supporters

First, a heartfelt thank you to the contributors—students, parents, and educators—who shared their stories, insights, and experiences. Your voices have brought this book to life and provided the foundation for all who read it. Your courage and openness have made this journey possible.

To the readers: thank you for your time, your engagement, and your willingness to reflect on your own journey. It is your commitment to growth that fuels this collective experience.

And to all those who supported the creation of this book—from the mentors who offered guidance to the families who provided love and strength—your role in this process has been invaluable. This book stands as a testament to your dedication and belief in the power of education and personal growth.

Special Contributors

Farai Ntuli

Purpose, compassion, and impact—these words encapsulate Farai Mubaiwa's dedication to shaping a better Africa. Farai serves as the Africa Livelihoods and Education Lead for Accenture Development Partnerships (ADP), where she addresses significant social, political, and economic challenges. Her previous roles include Chief Partnerships Officer at the Youth Employment Service (YES), Project Manager at The Aurum Institute, and analyst at Deloitte's Strategy and Operations Consulting.

Farai is also known for her influential blog series "Tips for Millennial Managers," co-founding the youth empowerment organization Afrika Matters, and her many accolades including the Queen's Young Leader for South Africa, TEDx speaker, One Young World Ambassador, King's Principal Global Leadership Award Recipient, Dalai Lama 2019 Fellow, and winner of the TransUnion Rising Star award (2022).

Her insightful contributions on entrepreneurship in this book bring valuable perspectives and practical wisdom that will inspire readers and enhance their journey toward growth and success.

Prof. Stephen James Heinrich Hendricks

This is a much-needed piece of scholarly work. Having recently retired from one of South Africa's historically disadvantaged universities, located in a semi-urban setting yet serving as a center of learning in the heart of Ga-Rankuwa, Mabopane, and Soshanguve, I can affirm that your analysis of the transition from high school to higher education, whether university or college, is completely accurate.

During my tenure as Dean of a health professional school, I found that many of my students were underprepared for the demands of first-year academic studies. Most were the first in their families to attend university, bearing the considerable pressure of high expectations from younger siblings and other family members. These expectations are addressed with great insight in this book.

Some students came from high school environments without laboratories or libraries. While they may have had a theoretical understanding of these academic structures, they had never engaged with science equipment or library resources during their school years. This reality highlights the importance of this book in helping such students successfully navigate the transition to higher education.

I value the term "Mother" in the book's title, as it is a deeply symbolic term. A "mother" may be a grandmother, aunt, or any family member who nurtured a student during their formative years. The "mother" can also represent the church or religious community from which a student comes, as well as the broader village or neighborhood that shaped them.

I suggest rephrasing the reference from "1 million learners" to "at least 1 million learners" because this book will also benefit second- and third-year higher education students who may have endured a very challenging first year at university or college.

Finally, I recommend considering a translation of this book into Afrikaans, a language spoken by many youth in communities of color as well as by white Afrikaner youth. Doing so would expand the book's reach and impact even further.

Recognize the Strength and Determination of All Participants

Each person who contributed to this book—from the students sharing their challenges to the parents offering their wisdom—has shown remarkable strength and determination. You have not only overcome difficulties, but you've also paved the way for others to follow in your footsteps.

Your resilience is an inspiration to others, and your stories prove that growth is possible, no matter the obstacles. Whether you are a student, a parent, or an educator, your journey matters, and your strength is a guiding light for future generations.

Encourage Readers to Practice Gratitude as a Tool for Growth

As you close this book, remember the power of gratitude. Take a moment each day to acknowledge the people who have helped you, the lessons you've learned, and the progress you've made. Gratitude isn't just about acknowledging what you have—it's about recognizing the support and opportunities that have shaped your journey.

Gratitude fosters a mindset of positivity, resilience, and growth. By making it a daily practice, you can transform your perspective and cultivate a life filled with appreciation and continuous learning.

Closing: A Journey of Hope

As we conclude this journey, it's important to remember that the story of your life is far from finished. Every step you've taken, every challenge you've faced, and every success, no matter how small, has contributed to the person you are today. It's easy to get caught up in the desire for immediate success or perfection, but true growth lies in the process itself.

Every chapter of your life, whether it's filled with triumph or hardship, is shaping you into a stronger, more resilient individual. The road to success is not linear, but it's the journey—both the highs and the lows—that builds character. As you continue to grow, learn, and evolve, remember that you are capable of handling whatever comes next.

This journey is not just about reaching a destination but about discovering who you are along the way. Take pride in your progress, and be patient with yourself as you move forward. You are building strength with every choice you make, and each experience adds to your wisdom.

Motivational Quote:

"Your story is still being written—embrace every chapter with courage and curiosity."

Your story isn't defined by a single event or moment. It's a collection of experiences, choices, and lessons. Don't rush through the chapters—embrace each one with an open heart and a willingness to learn. It's the curiosity to explore new opportunities and the courage to face challenges that will make your journey meaningful.